M000087066

THE WWII JOURNALS of E.J. BIRD

ILLUSTRATIONS BY E. J. BIRD

THE
WW
II
JOURNALS
of
E. J. BIRD

GIBBS·SMITH
P
PUBLISHER

SALT LAKE CITY

First Edition

03 02 01 3 2 1

Copyright for all text and artwork © 2001 by E. J. Bird
All rights reserved. No part of this book may be reproduced by any means whatsoever
without written permission from the publisher, except brief excerpts quoted for the purpose
of review.

Published by
Gibbs Smith, Publisher
P. O. Box 667
Layton, UT 84041
Orders: (1-800) 748-5439
Visit our Web site at www.gibbs-smith.com

Designed by Steven R. Jerman—Jerman Design Incorporated, Salt Lake City, Utah
Edited by Gail Yngve
Book printed in Hong Kong

Library of Congress Cataloging-in-Publication Data

Bird, E. J.
        The WW II journals of E. J. Bird / illustrations by E. J. Bird. — 1st ed.
            p.   cm.
        ISBN 1-58685-035-0
        1. Bird, E. J.—Diaries. 2. World War, 1939–1945—Personal narratives, American.
        3. United States. Army—Biography. 4. Artists—United States—Biography.
        5. World War, 1939–1945—Art and the war. I. Title: WW Two journals of E. J.
        Bird. II. Title: WW 2 journals of E. J. Bird. III. Title: World War II journals of E. J.
        Bird. IV. Title: World War Two journals of E. J. Bird. V. Title.
    D811.B515 A3 2001
    940.54'25'092—dc21
        [B]   00-063568

DEDICATION

TO RAY AND BETTY CHRISTENSEN,
DISTANT RELATIVES
AND CLOSE FRIENDS.

"BORED"

E.J. BIRD.

Preface

O F THE FEW ARTISTS WHO WERE WORKING IN THE 1940s and who are still creating today, one of the most venerable is E. J. Bird. He recently painted several outstanding oils and keeps his hands nimble through his creative drawings. Ultimately, his contribution to the art world will be seen in his insightful drawings of recent and past scenes.

Bird is a modest man not given to heroic gestures of epic proportion, yet history thrust him into two of the greatest American events of the twentieth century. The Great Depression found him heading the Utah WPA Federal Art Project, and World War II propelled him into fierce campaigns in the Pacific Theater. Both occasions saw him rise to the challenge as a man and as an artist.

His depression-era work has been well documented by my esteemed colleagues, Dr. Will South and Joanna Herndon, M.A., but his contributions during the war years have yet to be properly examined. In January of 1999, the Springville Museum of Art hosted a retrospective exhibition of Bird's oeuvre from the 1930s to 1999 and published a color-illustrated catalog and biography. The show was immensely popular and received critical acclaim.

Exhibited for the first time in recent years were two series of drawings done while he was a serviceman in World War II. The complete sets of San Francisco pen-and-ink drawings and pen-and-watercolor Okinawa drawings were at last seen together. Only after the exhibition did it come to light that an earlier cycle of pen-and-ink drawings depicting the USO during Bird's basic training existed. They, too, were filled with the same desperately rollicking character of the other sets.

In a conversation with his daughter, Robyn Lamm, we simultaneously spawned the idea of making a book of her father's "War Years" sketches. We felt that these drawings were not just shoot-'em-up combat pictures. They were true social narrative, contrasting uprooted GIs looking for a good time with war-weary refugees looking for safety. It was Bird's own very special view of the war he was conscripted to fight.

The idea was greeted with Bird's enigmatic smile and ambivalent acquiescence. "That's fine," he said, "but I am too old and too tired to do much work on it." He subsequently produced an original diary from those years and then personally wrote another seventy-five riveting pages of lively prose!

E.J. BIRD

But what is a book without a publisher? I recommended my friend Gibbs Smith, Utah's leading publisher of fine books. But Gibbs was not very interested at first. He rightly questioned the book's contribution to our understanding of the war, when it was actually the autobiography of a talented but lesser-known artist from Utah. What "bigger picture" did this book profess? My response:

This is not a book about E. J. Bird; it is about the predicament of millions of soldiers thrown together during difficult times. It is about life: ordinary men uprooted, trained, and sent into combat, sailors grabbing a fleeting respite with dance-hall floozies, and starving children begging for candy and cigarettes. It is not about one man but about a nation's loss of innocence, and it's all captured by one of its participants in an authentic journalistic fashion.

"Springfield MO, USO"

Gibbs saw the merit of this argument and the quality of the artwork itself, so he accepted the project. But just how good were these pen-and-ink drawings? In March of 1944, Charles Scribner's Sons published Aimée Crane's book *Art in the Armed Forces*, which at the time was the most complete book of war artists. Of these, Cpl. William J. Gunn, USMC, was closest in look and style to Bird of any of the artists. Other official pen-and-ink artists— Mitchell Jamieson, Herbert H. Laidman, Paul R. Ellsworth, Mauldin, and Harry A. Jackson— also approached E. J. Bird's artistic sensitivity.

However, it should be remembered that Bird was not an official war artist, just an ordinary soldier. His was the unofficial version of the war and was entirely personal. It did not relate to the war effort of the Special Service Division. We see a graphic artist who could not put down his pen just because he was doing something else. His noodling and doodling came from the inside out of an independent soul and was part and parcel of his expressive voice. His later illustrated books proved this point.

The sketches made are rare glimpses into a slice of life during those more turbulent times. They speak with clarity and immediacy of a time over half a century ago that is fast being lost to a personal memory. With pathos and humor, E. J. Bird's words and drawings tell an intimate story of one man's war, and the reader discovers the reality that was every man's war.

—*Vern G. Swanson—Director Springville Museum of Art*

GOD I HAVE THE FACILITY TO FORGET —
THUS MAKING THE WHOLE THING AS
SIMPLE AS TURNING THE PAGES OF
GOYA'S "HORRORS OF WAR."

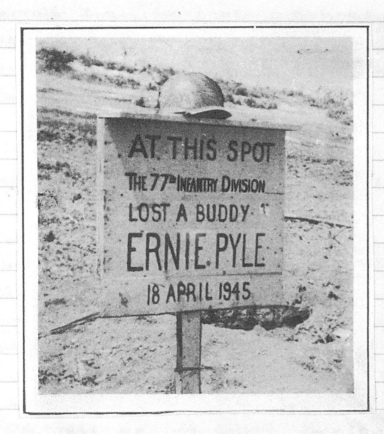

Introduction

IF A LIFE IS THE SUM OF ONE'S EXPERIENCES, then E. J. "Bill" Bird's life is as large as the West he has lived in for nine decades. He was a farm boy from 1917 to 1924; a teenager in the Roaring Twenties; a college man, artist, administrator, and husband against the backdrop of the Great Depression; a proud father and reluctant GI during World War II; an architectural draftsman and designer throughout the '50s, '60s, and '70s; a much-published author in the '80s and '90s; and still an artist when given a museum show in 1999. At the twentieth century's end, he could look back on a personal wealth of family and friends and claim, though his typical western modesty would not allow it, numerous contributions to the cultural wealth of his home state.

From 1929 to 1931, while a student at the University of Utah, Bill studied painting with Utah's most academically accomplished artist, James T. Harwood. It was a fortuitous meeting, as Bill learned from a master how to put paint on canvas and in the process made a true friend. The pair hiked, hunted, fished, and painted together, while Bill imbibed the lessons of sound draftsmanship as well as impressionist color. On more than one occasion, he put together paintings that looked incredibly close to the work of his much older Parisian-trained, Salon-recognized, award-winning mentor. He had, as he would later recall, "a good start" in art.

That good start was initially thwarted by the economic desperation of the 1930s. After a hopeful beginning working first for Utah artist Jack Sears in 1931 and then for Walt Disney in southern California in 1933, he was laid off and found himself back in Utah with two dollars in his pocket. Along with his wife, Nan Fugate Bird, whom he had married in 1932, Bill remained positive. He continued to study art, including etching with Harwood, and gave lessons in outdoor drawing to private pupils. But that did not provide nearly enough money to live on. When President Roosevelt's alphabet-soup programs came along, Bill found himself digging up dirt for the Public Works Administration, established in March 1933. This was the time that his refined-sounding name, Elzy, gave way to the more rough-and-ready nickname of Bill.

It was the Roosevelt public works projects, however, that took the shovel out of Bill's hand and put the brush back in it. In the winter of 1933–34, the Public Works of Art Project was established, followed in 1935 by the Works Projects Administration's Federal Art Project (FAP). Bill participated in both, first as an artist, then as a director of the FAP for the state of Utah.

These years were exciting and productive for Bill. He was involved with and/or oversaw projects as various as the publishing of the *Index of American Design* and the first edition of *Utah: A Guide to the State*, the building of the Utah State Art Center and the administration of its school,

E. J. BIRD.

"Floozies"

the founding of several rural art centers, the documenting of pictographs and petroglyphs in the Barrier Canyon Project, the hosting of many national traveling exhibitions, and the continuous promoting of homegrown talent. He also managed to dance the night away once in awhile at Saltair to the music of the big bands. His experience of the Great Depression was, we might conclude with the blinders of the present, counterintuitive; he was happy.

"Beginning of a Large Evening"

Bill's art and his own attitude typified something essential about the history of Utah art with its emphasis on optimism and its propensity to choose the picturesque over pain and poverty because of the widely held Utah belief that honest labor saves us from these ills. To this cultural tradition he often added a subtle strain of mirth. His 1938 watercolor *Takin' Five* is a telling work of art. In it, he suggests that one must work, of course, but one must also pull over and daydream or have a smoke or a nap under a huge shade tree. He understood work and he understood play, undertaking expressions of each with a wry sense of humor.

In his 1940 oil painting *The Gossips*, he poked fun at small-mindedness and conformity. The rather unattractive rural residents depicted had more to sit on than think about, the artist rightly observed. Not surprisingly, given its forthright quality, small-mindedness followed the picture like tin cans tied to a Model T. Despite its debut in a major exhibition, installed between a Thomas Hart Benton and a Grant Wood, *The Gossips* was subsequently excluded from the Springville Museum of Art's 1940 salon. In the early 1980s, there was still too much maximus in the picture's collective gluteus for public propriety and again it was rejected, this time for purchase. In an act of artistic contrition, it was the Springville Museum of Art that sponsored Bill's 1999 one-person show. *The Gossips* was reproduced in full color on the cover of the show's catalog, a welcome irony not lost on the artist.

The "good times" of the 1930s, as Bill recalls them, ended with the onset of World War II. He was drafted and eventually caught up in the invasion of Okinawa. Even during these horrific days, Bill found a way to deal constructively and creatively with his experiences. He made drawings of wartime scenes, of soldiers and floozies and the tragically dispossessed. These drawings are a record of one man's view of a sometimes amusing, sometimes frightening, but always interesting world, and they are the subject of this delightful volume.

I met Bill Bird and his wife, Nan, in 1981 on the occasion of a small exhibition in Bountiful, Utah, that I had organized, entitled *Utah Art: The Early Years*. The Birds had come out to see the works by James T. Harwood then on display, and we struck up a conversation about the artist. They suggested I come over for coffee, which I did, and that was the first among many, many more visits.

My curiosity about Harwood turned into a book project. Based on no evidence whatsoever, Bill and Nan never questioned that I could write it. They patiently answered question after question, tempering a good many of my youthful overestimations with their calm sense of fairness. Bill, especially, could spin yarns about the past that made Harwood come alive for me, and, in a very real sense, he helped bring the life and art of his old friend and teacher back to the attention of the Utah public.

That book came out and visits to the Birds' house continued, along with coffee, cake, conversation, and bourbon balls at Christmastime. And there were more publications: Bill's gift for combining tall tales and lively drawings resulted in one beautifully illustrated children's book after another. He always found time, too, to help me with various art histories that never could have been written without his help, including the first-ever article on the Utah FAP and, most recently, on depression-era printmakers in Utah (a catalog for which he penned a colorful introduction). He wrote me once from New York that he was entitled to "at least share in the P of your Ph.D."

Over the past twenty years of coffee and collaboration, Bill rarely alluded to his World War II experiences. I knew about the drawings he had made then but did not know until quite recently that he had also kept a wartime journal. He mentioned it in passing, and a keen desire to read it swelled in me. But I managed (uncharacteristically) to refrain from questioning him about something so personal. Perhaps sensing the right time had come, he loaned it to me, and its freshness, simplicity, and honesty were a revelation. Bill's knack for capturing the human element of time and place with an ever-present gentle humor was there.

Bill's daughter, Robyn, was aware of the journal and the wartime drawings, too. Knowing all about her dad's storytelling abilities, she advocated a memoir to go along with the drawings and envisioned yet another book. I seconded her enthusiasm. Taking on the project with some small trepidation (after all, he wasn't seventy anymore, he told me, and this thing was going to require some energy), Bill wrote the following memoir in longhand (as he writes everything) over the course of several months of silent afternoons spent in his well-worn living room chair.

The result is, like his more private journal, a series of word pictures that, along with his drawings, describe in a plain, personal, and compelling way the atmosphere enveloping one of America's defining moments. It is also a glimpse into the tough, witty, sweet, talented, generous, and whimsical personality of its author, a man who has given so much back to his family, friends, community, and country for so long that it is all the more an honor to be able to say thank you, Bill, for your talents, gifts, and memories.

—Will South—Curator of Collections, Weatherspoon Art Gallery

E.J.BIRD.

"Downtown"

"No Beer
Tonight"

E.J. BIRD

World War II Remembered

I DISCOVERED THAT IF A PERSON LIVES LONG ENOUGH, it eventually occurs to him that everything coming his way—good luck or adversity—is only a temporary thing. For instance, the Great Depression only lasted from 1929 until the early forties when World War II preempted it, and thank God it was only a temporary thing. World War II, though, lasted a shorter period of time but seemed to go on forever.

Hitler's year was 1939. Germany's armies surging through Europe had overrun every country on the continent except Russia. The English Channel was the only barrier keeping them from taking England. In December of 1941, the Japanese, wanting a piece of the action, bombed our Pearl Harbor in Hawaii, and the United States found itself embroiled in this wild mix of warfare both in Europe and in the Pacific. So here we were, thrust from the cocoon of isolationism into a world being torn violently apart by two little men—Hitler, with his comic Charlie Chaplin mustache, and Tojo, with his squinty eyes. Ironically, both men were small in stature, yet they both had enormous egos.

This was not just any war; this was the big one! Every United States citizen was somehow involved. The rules came from Washington: ALL men age eighteen through thirty-five must register for the draft. Gasoline and certain types of food were strictly rationed. Money wasn't all that was needed to buy a pair of shoes; one needed a certain piece of paper, too, for Washington was in charge, sometimes even making rules for their rules.

For me the timing was crummy. I had begun to prove myself as a fine artist who deserved the title "fine." I was being invited to exhibit, not only locally but on a national level, and for several years had been the State Director of the WPAs Federal Art Project in Utah, with eighty people working under my direction. I had a great staff and we were involved in easel and mural paintings for public buildings, exhibitions, and art classes. I was on the Board of Directors of the Utah State Institute of Fine Arts. I had been married to my lovely wife since 1932, and we were making payments on our first home.

At thirty-one, I was practically an old man, but according to the rules—those Washington Rules—if a man was of the proper age and gender, he must register for the draft. He would be excused from service only if his job contributed to the war effort, if he had children, if he was enrolled in college, or if he was in some way physically or mentally inept. As with every war, there were dissidents, draft dodgers, and perpetual students piling up one degree after another.

Fven after I went before the draft board for my physical and the oral and written I.Q. and dexterity tests, I thought, I'm too old. They'll never take me. I'm too old! In December of 1942, I was being fitted for a uniform and assigned a bunk in a barrack at Fort Douglas, Utah. At that time there were several million of us in uniform, and each one of us was affected differently. I had been a happy civilian and would have been much happier staying that way. To begin with, I was not the macho type. My tendency was to stay in the background, trying not to make waves. I had sensitive hands and a more sensitive nose and wasn't one to punch my way into any situation where I'd come out bloody, but nobody in the army asked me how I felt about being in the army.

I was assigned a double bunk, one of a pair off in one corner of the barrack. I looked around at my companions and exchanged names with them. Opposite me, top and bottom, were a thirty-two-year-old Basque sheepherder from the desert country out near Tooele, Utah, and a thirty-four-year-old transient from New Mexico. In the top bunk over my head was a one-eyed road builder from Moab, Utah, and he was, indeed, a character. He told us his road crew was made up mostly of Indians from his area. Every time he took off for town to pick up supplies, he'd come back and find the whole crew hunkered down in the shade of the junipers. Finally he decided he'd "fix 'em," so the next time he left, he removed his glass eye from its socket and set it on a rock. "I'll be watching you while I'm gone," he said. When he returned, they hadn't "missed a lick!" I've often wondered what happened to this guy. He should have wound up a bird colonel or at least first sergeant. Anyway, when I looked at these characters, I realized that when they got around to drafting me, the army was really scraping the bottom of the barrel.

"Top
 Sergeant"

At that time, Fort Douglas was a preliminary processing unit serving the Intermountain area. Here is where the fact that I was no longer a civilian really sank in. It seemed organized confusion when we were herded from one area to another in the jumble of old buildings for medical shots, fittings in dress uniforms, fatigues, and shoes. We were piled high with blankets, toilet kits, field packs, and barrack bags—all the things needed for army living. In addition, we were fingerprinted and given registration numbers on metal dog tags. Mine was 39903806, and I'll never, ever forget it. In a seating area, we sat and filled out forms while disinterested guys with clipboards asked stupid questions, some even having to do with our love lives. At the end was a mailing room, a place filled with boxes and wrapping paper where we could mail our civilian clothes and possessions home.

After breakfast the next morning, a sergeant came through the barracks with a clipboard. "The following men will gather up all your gear and bedding. You will form a double line outside and wait for me." Those of us whose names were on the roster found trucks waiting. We were loaded in and told we were being taken across town to Kearns. A half-hour south and west of Salt Lake City there was a flat windblown area given to dry-farm wheat and pasturelands. In 1942, it was reached by a winding country road, and this is where the army built the new base of Kearns. It was way down on my list as a place to visit, much less a place for spending any significant time. At first, I saw only row upon row of tar-paper barracks, each with a small appendage housing the latrine. All of them were long and squat with low-pitched ridged roofs. Everything exposed to the outside weather, except a door at one end and three small windows spaced high on either side, was covered with black tar paper. There were several larger brick buildings, some for administrative functions, some for mess halls. Altogether it was a desolate place with a certain similarity to the moon.

Two surly guards let us through the gate, and our truck came to a stop before an empty barrack. Before we were even unloaded, I heard it—the "F" word. The army somehow thought they invented it, but they hadn't. Even as a kid herding pigs on the farm, I had heard it used, and two summers working on cattle ranches near Idaho's Snake River and two more summers working on construction gangs had seasoned me to all the four-letter words. This, though, was different. They savored it and played with it, used it as a noun, as a verb, as an adjective, and as an adverb, sometimes even in the same sentence. Here in the drill field next to where we had stopped, an agitated red-necked sergeant brought his marching platoon to a halt. I could tell he was displeased because of his sharp jerky movements and because of the way he glared. He drew his body up as if his clothes were too tight, then let it loose in a sudden explosion. Ripping off his hat, he threw it on the ground and jumped up and down on it, hollering, "I'll be a f—-ing motherf—-ing f—-er!" I thought then, and still do, that this was a classic and very special expletive, one that indicated when a person was really p—-ed off. Even after I became a first sergeant myself, I used it only on special occasions.

After unloading, we had our first look inside the barrack. Truthfully, it was no more impressive than the outside. Our new home had a rough wooden floor, exposed unpainted studs and rafters, and I could see black insulation board on the walls and plywood sheathing on the roof. The room must have been at least twenty-two feet wide and eighty feet long because it was planned primarily for a platoon of thirty-two men and two noncoms. At right angles to the walls, on both sides and spaced maybe five feet apart, were empty canvas folding cots. Next to every other cot was a half-gallon can from the kitchen for cigarette butts, and at eye level along the side walls, shelves and hooks had been placed for hanging and storing clothes. In the center aisle, room was made for two small potbellied stoves with coal buckets and kindling. Four exposed lightbulbs dangled from the ceiling rafters on naked cords. I could tell from the leftover smells that our new home had been lived in before; stale coal and tobacco smoke, dirty socks, and body odors permeated the barrack. This was just one step above living in tents and certainly no Ritz-Carlton.

The sergeant who had accompanied us in the trucks showed us just how to spread our blankets on the cots and where to stow our gear along the walls, then he gave us half an hour to change into fatigues before dinner. In the army, we had dinner at noon and supper in the evening. There were several mess halls at Kearns, huge places that could serve five hundred men at one sitting. At each meal a thousand men were served cafeteria style on compartmented aluminum trays. The food was not fancy, but it was edible, and after I got used to it, I actually looked forward to it.

Kearns was a place of orientation, a place of change from civilian to soldier. I'd had several years of ROTC in high school and college, so I knew what to expect. We had long hours of close-order drill and days of tromping in line. "Fall in. Column right, march. Hut, two, three, four. Column left, march. To the rear, march. Hut, two, three, four." Each time out, we drilled until the drill sergeant got tired. Close-order drill is a monotonous way to spend a morning or an afternoon or both. We'd be going along pretty well when someone would make a mistake. Then we were halted and chewed out for ten minutes or so by the drill sergeant, and it started again. Hut, two, three, four. Hut, two, three, four.

Reveille was at six A.M. The tar-paper latrines were supposedly built to accommodate all thirty-four men in the barrack, but the guy who designed them had arbitrarily decided that there would be ten guys using the urinal trough, ten sitting on the toilets, which were lined up side-by-side and spaced at exactly twenty-four inches center-to-center, and ten guys shaving at one wall of hung basins with tiny individual mirrors. This would leave four guys waiting. In

"SCRUB DETAIL"

E.J. BIRD—

reality the designer had no idea what thirty-four guys would do when turned loose all at the same time with a limited time span. Not a clue. First off, seventeen or eighteen guys would be trying for the urinal trough. There would be one or two sitting on the johns. The rest would be elbowing each other for space at the basins, trying to brush their teeth and shave, using the old Gillette blue blades and soap that needed water to make it foam. After the initial urinal rush, approximately three guys would crowd each basin at the same time. No one took a shower in the morning. We saved that for after supper, being allowed only fifteen minutes before we had to be lined up for breakfast. One can imagine what the latrine looked like after that fifteen minutes.

The army has no lower rank than a private, unless it's a private on KP, which stands for Kitchen Police. There's no "police" about it, it's just sloppy work around the kitchen and mess halls. In Kearns, they decided somehow that they needed twenty to thirty men on KP to operate each of their mess halls, and they chose our whole platoon for it. KP began at four A.M. each day, two hours before reveille. Once in the light of the mess hall, they lined us up and inspected us to see that we'd shaved and had clean fingernails. Separated into smaller crews we were given our assignments for the day. "You, help the cooks. You, grab those mops. I want the whole mess hall mopped before breakfast. You, wipe down the tables and fill the salt and pepper shakers. You and you, you're dishwashers for the day. Grab those pots. You, find soap and brushes at the sinks." The chores went on and on until after breakfast. It's a lot of work to feed five hundred men in one place at one time and to feed one thousand per meal, three times each day. It would've taken a herd of cattle to feed each one a steak for supper, but four sides of beef made a stew or hash to feed the whole bunch. So we were fed a steady diet of stew and hash, and sometimes for breakfast we got salty-tasting canned chipped beef mixed with milk gravy on toast that we called "s--t on a shingle."

Those helping the cooks found themselves serving. We were armed with spoons and ladles and lined up behind the long serving counter with its pans of hot and cold food. As the men came down the counter, sliding their trays, we would dish out the stew, potatoes, gravy, and mixed vegetables. We could get a whole bunch through the line in a hurry that way.

I mentioned before that in civilian life I'd been an executive type, making decisions that were carried out by people under me. One time I forgot that I was the lowliest of the low (a private on KP). I was serving gravy next to a big linebacker sort who was serving mashed potatoes. Here comes a little skinny guy, pushing his tray. Plop. Mashed potatoes. He looked up and said, "Give me a little more, please."

"One scoop's all you get. That's the rules," said the linebacker. I had already served him his gravy. Without thinking I reached over with my empty ladle, dipped into the potato pan, and put a blob on his tray. I reloaded my scoop with gravy and found the linebacker in my face, waving his spoon at me and hollering, "Why'd you do that? I told him one scoop!"

Things started to get ugly. I think there were only two things that kept it from turning into a brawl. One, I was waving my scoop of hot gravy back at him, and two, a bunch of hollering GIs on the other side of the counter were acting very much like they wanted a piece of the action. He backed down. Later, as I tried to figure out what'd happened, it occurred to me that the potatoes belonged to the army, and the skinny kid belonged to the army, so what's the difference if he'd got the whole pan?

It took only a short while to figure out the army's way of operating. The fellows in the next barrack were alternating with us. They were going through their close-order drill while we were on KP. They were outside, and we were inside; the next day we reversed. The concept was okay, but it didn't take into account the December weather, which can be tricky in the Salt Lake Valley. This was a year when it got freezing cold. It would snow all one day and leave about twelve inches on the ground, then warm up enough to melt it all, leaving the drill fields at Kearns about six inches deep in gumbo mud. After slopping in it up to our knees one day, the drill sergeant said he'd see what he could do.

A word about our winter clothing: we all had one of the cool caps like the character Radar O'Reilly wore on the television series M*A*S*H, one that would pull down over our ears. We also had cotton underwear like the character Hawkeye and fatigues made from heavy cloth almost like denim but not as heavy. We each had pants, a shirt, and a lined jacket, all the same khaki color. There were no zippers in World War II; everything buttoned. We wore wool gloves and heavy leather, laced ankle-high shoes.

DEAR BETTY —
    WHEN I
CAME IN THE
ARMY ALL THEY
DID WAS SHOOT
ME — MAINLY IN
THE ARMS — THAT
IS THE ONLY
REASON I
CAN THINK OF
WHY THEY MADE
ME A CORPORAL —
SO THAT THE
CHEVERONS
WOULD COVER
UP THE HOLES. IT WAS
HARDER ON THE BIG FELLOWS
AT FIRST — BECAUSE THEY
FELL HARDER — DID
YOU EVER HEAR OF
THE "BLUE ARMY"?
THAT'S HOW THEY GOT
THAT WAY.

    I'M NOT
GIVING AWAY
ANY MILITARY
SECRETS WHEN
I SAY THAT THE ARMY OWNS 4709560321780995
10000 7694321 467181984378⅞ PANS AND
POTS. I WASHED, SCRAPED AND SCOURED
4321643 POTS AND TWO TEASPOONS — THAT'S WHY
I HAD A VERY BAD CASE OF DISHPAN HANDS —
THE ARMY CURES THIS BY MAKING YOU WASH
MORE POTS AND PANS.

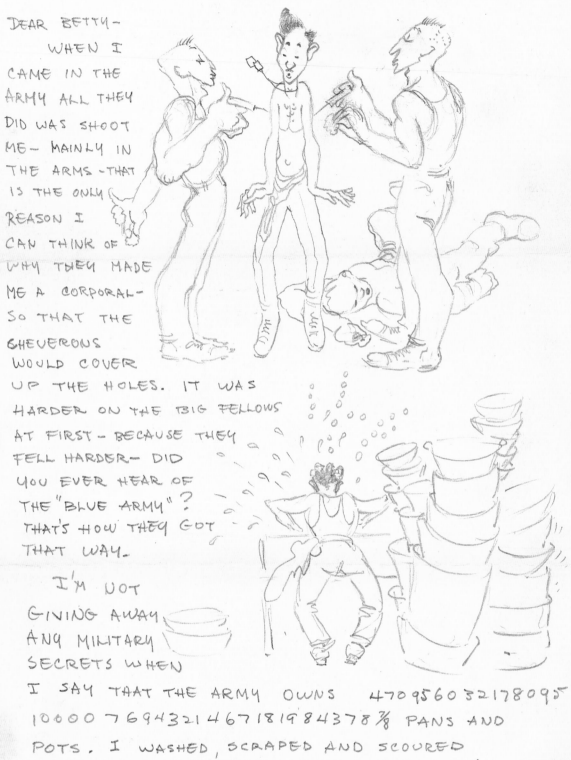

ANOTHER THING —
I FOUND OUT
WHY THEY
MARCH YOU
AROUND SO MUCH
IS TO GET YOUR HIPS BACK IN PLACE AFTER SLEEPING
ON THOSE HARD BEDS. I GOT SO I WOULD
GET THE GUARD TO WAKE ME UP AT MIDNITE
AND TURN ME OVER — TO KEEP MY SPINE STRAIGHT.

WE ALSO LEARNED HOW TO USE
A BAYONET. THE IDEA WAS TO
LOOK VERY UGLY AND FEROCIOUS —
AFTER DRILL ONE DAY THE SARGENT
LOOKED AT MY FACE AND SAID:
"ALL RIGHT, BIRD, PRACTICE IS OVER, YOU
DON'T HAVE TO GO AROUND LOOKING
UGLY ALL THE TIME!" WE STARTETED
OUT WITH RUBBER BAYONETS AND
GRADUALLY WORKED UP TO THE HARDER
ONES MADE OF STEEL. THEY
BOUNCE RIGHT OFF NOW —
WONT THE JAPS BE
SURPRISED!

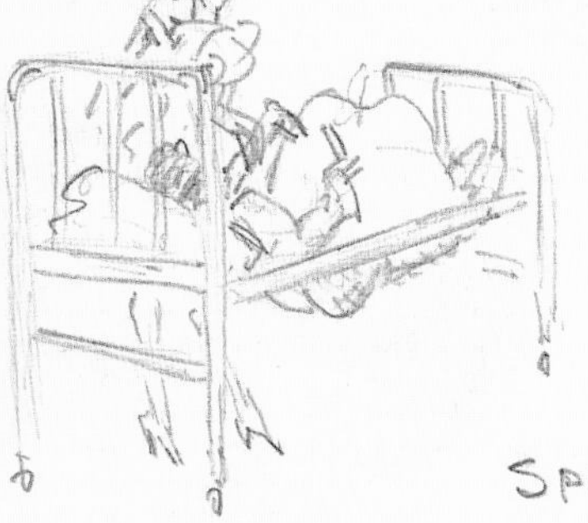

WELL — I FINALLY LANDED
IN THE HOSPITAL — AND AS
YOU CAN SEE — THE ONLY
REASON I AM STAYING
ON IS BECAUSE THEY HAVE
SPRINGS ON THE BED.
YOURS
Bill

When we first came to Kearns, there weren't enough rifles to go around, so we were each issued a wooden replica. This was a one-inch board cut in the shape of the old army Springfield thirty-caliber rifle used in World War I. This, they told us, was not for shooting but strictly for use in drill. I was happy about this. The old Springfield weighed ten pounds. I had used one in high school and knew that it would weigh more like thirty after I'd carried it for a whole day.

"Chow Line- Rainy Day"

The GI shoes were comfortable and heavy, but the army had nothing that would navigate in gumbo mud and we were surprised at the solution. The evening before our next day on the drill field, a truck stopped at our door and delivered a pile of GI overshoes. They had black rubber bottoms and buckled fabric tops that came halfway up to the knees. The sergeant told us each to pick out a pair that fit, then went off laughing. We found out why when we pawed through the pile. They were all size fourteen.

Next morning we were all set for the blowing sleet in our faces and the gumbo mud: wool caps pulled way down, heavy jackets pulled way up, wool gloves, wooden stick rifles on our shoulders, and everyone in overshoes that felt like we had a rowboat on each foot. The sergeant smiled when he hollered, "Fall in! I want you to look sharp now."

This had gone on for three weeks: on-again-off-again drill field and KP. Then it was Christmas. I somehow got a two-day pass and relatives came to pick me up in my own '36 Ford. My sweet wife, Nan, had a tree set up in our living room, a turkey, and presents—everything that made Christmas special. It was good to sleep in my own bed next to my sweet-smelling spouse. It sure beat the hell out of the hard canvas cot in the smoke-filled barrack. December twenty-fifth, December twenty-sixth, then back to the army again. Christmas 1942 was over.

When the army wanted to move a large number of men from one place to another, they used troop trains or troop ships. My experience with the ships came later, but I was about to have my first with a train. The army went to the railroad bone yard and selected one of those old-time steam engines, the ones with the cowcatcher in front, preferably one with flat wheels. It had all the goodies on top—a bell that jangled when the proper chain was pulled and a steam whistle that sounded like a lone wolf on a cold night when another chain was pulled. The engine was equipped with an attached coal car, a big boiler, and a couple of shovels.

Digging deeper in the bone yard, the army found four old Pullman cars and one odd express car, then they found four more of the Pullmans. They weren't too fussy, only checking to be sure that the wheels were tightly fitted to the carriages so the trains wouldn't jump the tracks. They also checked to make sure the steam pipes for heating still worked. If they leaked a little, it was okay, but they couldn't leak too much. In addition, they checked to see if the upper bunks still pulled down, and if there was a mattress in both upper and lower bunks. The troops had their own blankets.

They took the old express car and stripped it of everything, right down to the floor boards, built a flat sandbox in the middle to install an army field kitchen, and knocked a hole in the roof for the field-kitchen stovepipe. Now we had a diner. We were ready to roll.

I was issued a mess kit when they were handing out the uniforms. A mess kit is an oval aluminum pan, maybe nine inches long and one-and-a-half inches deep. It has an attached handle that folds over a convex lid and locks. Inside are a knife, fork, and spoon, also aluminum. They don't fit anyplace and rattle pretty well when the kit is shaken. The lid has a couple of loops in the bottom and a slight crease running its length on top. This is so the folding handle of the kit can be run through the loops when the bottom, or concave, side of the lid is up. Thus, with the main kit in the left hand, the lid can be balanced on an arm, creating a two-compartment gadget for receiving food and eating it when standing up.

Our first supper on the train went okay, as did breakfast, but dinner at noon was another story. My bunk was in the number-two car. Along came a line of men from the last four cars. The line went through our car and ended in the number-one car. This is so the last man in the number-eight car had cleared the diner. The line reversed itself on signal and marched past the servers in the diner then on to their seats, each with a full mess kit.

Then it was our turn, and our line headed for the rear of the train. This was simple.

"Train Station"

We'd done it at supper and at breakfast. The food had been edible, but the service left something to be desired. At noon it was different. The cooks got carried away and prepared spaghetti and pickled beets. Just imagine a line of men in the aisles of those old Pullmans, mess trays of spaghetti and beets balanced on their arms. Every time the train lurched, food spilled down our fronts and onto the floor. We soon found out that spaghetti is a slippery food and can sure as hell mess things up.

This was my first New Year's Eve in the army, and when I spread my blankets in the upper bunk, I felt very low . . . and very sick. A lot of it had to do with the high smell of the sour food spread around. We were somewhere in Colorado, going east. I didn't know where we were headed.

I lay there until the next afternoon when we had reached our destination, which turned out to be O'Riley General Hospital in Springfield, Missouri. We were told that we were to be there for some time, that we were assigned to the Medical Corps, and that this was to be our place of training. We were all to be made corporals. Thank God! No more KP.

Exposing us to the raw outside winds of Kearns' drill fields one day and the steamy mess halls for the next four weeks hadn't done the troops much of a favor. Seven of us were taken off the train on stretchers. Six of us were placed in a hospital ward with fevers of 104 degrees and strep throats. The seventh was taken to the morgue.

E.J.B.
"DETAIL" O'REILLY GEN
HOSPITAL
FEB-10-'43

"More Chiefs than Indians"

I'll say this for the doctors and staff at O'Riley General Hospital: they knew what they were doing. Penicillin was just coming into use then. What with that and the loving care of several pretty nurses, they had me on my feet in two or three days. I found that they were keeping me for a week so they could monitor the penicillin treatment just as a precaution. Then the fellow in the next bunk was diagnosed with scarlet fever. The whole ward, which contained maybe twenty soldiers, was quarantined for thirty days! This was a lousy time. We were all well except this one guy. How do twenty people cope with being penned up in a small area with just room for the bunks and a minimum john?

Several card games were going on, and when one guy had all the money, we started playing for matches. The nurses brought us books and magazines. Somehow—at the time it seemed forever—the thirty days were up, and we were finally free again.

Of all the places where I would be assigned in the next three years, this was the most plush. The large two-story barrack had hardwood floors and central heating. Part of the lower floor was given to a large latrine area. I had come here after class had been in session for a couple of days, but they found a place for me on the second floor in a small private room. Bear in mind, this barrack was now a school, and the barrack was used more as dormitories than to house troops. The little room normally would be occupied by the first sergeant and maybe his clerk. This room had three bunks, two of which were occupied by kosher Jewish boys from the Bronx. They seemed okay, and I knew we'd get along.

Being at O'Riley was like being away at a college. My days consisted of classrooms and labs presided over by a civilian doctor turned major. I wish I could, but after fifty-plus years, I can't recall his name, so he'll have to remain "major." The course could have been called Army Med Tech 101. Although I never could stand the sight of blood, here I was . . . starting to become a medical technician. I found out later that it was because I'd had a couple of years of college chemistry. The army had mysterious ways of making their assignments. I'd had college courses with lab work, so this wasn't entirely new to me. I enjoyed the course, and the major was a good instructor.

Although I was surrounded by many people, this was a lonesome time for me. I missed my sweet wife. I really missed her. We were mostly free in the evenings and on weekends, and I found that going to town helped a little. Springfield was a sizeable midwestern town, and I discovered a restaurant where I could get a delicious corn-fed beefsteak. I think this was the best beef I'd ever tasted. It was tender, not stringy like our western range-fed cattle. Springfield had movie theaters and a bar or two where I could sit and have a lonesome beer, and there was also the local USO. That was where the action was. They had some jukebox music, music of the times, jumping music of the big bands—Tommy Dorsey, Kay Kaiser, Vince Lombardo, and Sammy Kaye—all playing I-miss-my-wife kind of music. The dance of the day was the jitterbug, and if a soldier didn't know how, the pretty girls of the USO would be more than willing to teach him.

My life settled for a while. It seemed somewhat better. Mess-hall food took on a more southern flavor: honey ham, black-eyed peas, sweet potatoes, corn bread. It beat the hell out of what we had at Kearns. Maybe too it only seemed better because there was no KP. Instead of

"Springfield
MO, USO"

E.J.Bird

E. J. Bird.

smelling like Kearns' coal smoke, my clothes took on a much different flavor. Cooped up in my small room in the handsome barrack, it took me some time to realize that my flavor was now "kosher." I learned early on that my Jewish roommates both had Jewish mothers. Packages of Jewish food kept arriving through the mail. I found what it was like to be stuck in a small room with lox and bagels and kosher meats of all kinds. Kosher salami gets pretty rank with no refrigeration. After three days in the mail and a couple more in a warm room, lox is pretty limp, but the salami takes on extra strength as the days go by. When we were inspected every Saturday morning by white-gloved officers, I knew they were suspicious. They sniffed a lot when they came in, yet they never discovered the source of the wild smells. My friends had the goodies safely tucked away in the ceiling access to the attic above our heads.

One Saturday I dropped into a local Woolworth's and purchased some art supplies and began sketching. I'd found out early on that I wasn't a gambler, which was how most of the soldiers occupied evenings, but I could sketch them. I spent a lot of my time sketching what I saw. This helped pass the lonesome evenings. I think I sketched merely to pass the time, and a lot of the drawings were given away or tossed in the garbage. I took my sketchbook with me to the USO. The wild dancing—the way the kids threw each other around— intrigued me and was recorded in my book. From then on, all through my time in the army, I found this was one way to keep me from going nuts from the boredom.

While at Kearns, I'd called my wife every evening. There was a pay phone near the mess hall, and I'd keep it warm for a half an hour or so. At O'Riley, I'd call once or twice each week, and I'd write her notes and send them frequently. I'd write my friends and relatives and looked forward to mail call every evening just before suppertime.

I enjoyed my stay at O'Riley. If I had to be away from my home and family, this was much better than mucking through the winter months with the infantry like some of my friends were doing. A good deal of the lab and class time was spent identifying certain diseases. Under the microscope, for instance, the pneumonia cell was an elongated oval shape with a dark center nucleus. When adding urine to a beaker of a certain solution, it would turn

"Odd Man Out"

E.J.BIRD

yellow if diabetes was present. Of course, one could expect some not-too-bright kid to slip a sugar cube into the beaker as a perverse joke, and the solution would turn a bright sunflower color. We always tested our own urine, so this would come as quite a shock. I was given a dead mouse once, and I was to determine what disease had killed him. So I'd get some of his blood and make a slide, then use the microscope. My mouse was pinned to the table and my scalpel

E.J.BIRD-

had made a neat cut down his belly. Wanting to produce enough blood for a slide, I dragged the scalpel through the cut again and found that the tip of my little finger had tracked through the cut preceding the scalpel. Then I found that my mouse had died of pneumonia, and for several days I was certain that my finger was in a high state of contamination.

We were tested. Bucking for a good mark I added some artwork to my paper drawings of various cells in relation to red and white blood cells. When my paper was returned, I had an excellent mark and my major asked me to see him in his office after class. He first complimented me on my drawings then asked if I'd be interested in doing some teaching-aid posters that he could use in his classes. He also asked if I'd be willing to come in the evening so as not to interfere with the schoolwork. I jumped at the chance, and he set me up with the materials I would need. I explained that this would take some weeks, and it did. As I remember, there were eight or ten posters in full color. When I'd finished, I called on him, and we sat and looked at them in his office. The major was a doctor first. Not much of the military had rubbed off on him. "Bird," he said, "what the hell are you doing in the Medical Corps when you can draw like this?"

"I wish I knew, Sir. I go where they send

me and hope for better times."

"Maybe I can help. Do you mind if I give it a try?"

In a week or so he called me, and we talked again. "There's an outfit forming out on the West Coast. It will be what they call a Headquarters Company, and they'll be making maps and posters for the air force. It sounds right up your alley and I can arrange a transfer if you'd like."

This sounded a lot better to me than where I was headed in the medics, so I told him to go ahead. I didn't relish the idea of tromping through North Africa with one of Patton's outfits, chasing and being chased by the Germans under Rommel. Within a week I was on a train and on my way to sunny California.

To take a train anywhere in the United States in 1943 was truly an adventure. The railroads must never have destroyed a Pullman car since they'd started making them early in the eighteen hundreds. They even smelled like mothballs. This old baby I rode from Springfield, Missouri, down across the panhandle of Texas and into California was a real beauty with plush red velvet seats and red tassels on the window blinds. The woodwork was light polished oak, and the carpet on the floor featured large red roses. The heating system was a lovely old potbellied stove with lots of brass work showing—even a brass-covered coal bucket. I almost expected a feather-bed when they made them up for the evening; but no, it was like all other Pullman mattresses, only this one, I think, was lumpier. The end of the line for me was Riverside, California, a large military airfield south of San Bernardino.

It took them three days to figure out I'd been delivered to the wrong base. The outfit I was looking for was at Hamilton Field, north of San Francisco. I took that leg of the journey by bus. Nowadays, a person can take a plane, and it's only twenty hours from Minneapolis to Australia, but in 1943, it took me that long on the bus to go from lower California to the Bay Area.

Hamilton Field was a well-established airfield just north of San Rafael. It was a busy place the latter part of March 1943, and I was directed to a group of temporary barracks made of plywood and canvas. The weather here at that time of year was very mild. I was met by my new first sergeant, who welcomed me to the "914 Engineer Air Force Headquarters Company." I was assigned to a platoon and shown to my bunk. I found out soon enough that this was more like the real army than my previous hitch with the medics. This, I thought, was a mapmaking, poster-making outfit, but I soon learned that those tasks were far down the road. Six o'clock was reveille, then calisthenics, breakfast, close-order drill—this time with the new

"Head of Market Street, San Francisco"

M1 rifle—dinner, and maybe a five-mile hike. If I went out the gate and crossed the busy highway to the west, I came to a dirt road that wound up the rolling side hills. This brought me to a high, flat, rolling country of cow pastures, fields and wildflowers, winding creeks, and, of all things, a small herd of white-tailed deer. How could such a beautiful wild place exist not twenty-five miles north of one of the largest cities in America? It was a nice place to hike, and the 914th used it several times each week.

In very little time, I discovered that several of the fellows left each night. They took the bus to San Rafael, where they stayed with their wives, then rode back to camp each morning by bus in time for reveille. Well, now. Okay! This was a new wrinkle. I obtained official permission and called Nan. She was all excited, and it was soon arranged. I got a weekend pass and met her at the bus station in San Francisco.

Everybody has certain times in life when things happen that will never be forgotten. This was one of those times for me. I remember the hotel, an old place on Grant Street near Chinatown, and the flower stall where we stopped to buy a white gardenia. The old woman pinned it on Nan's jacket, then turned to me. "I can see you two are really in love." She pinned

"The Big Spenders"

another white gardenia on my uniform jacket. "This one is my gift to you," she said.

We found an Italian place to eat—a place with snow-white linen on the table, Lenox china, and sterling silverware. The forks were lined up on the left side of the plate—far more forks than I would ever use at one sitting. Soft Italian violin music was playing somewhere in the background and two tuxedoed waiters hovered nearby, bound to please and really working for their gratuity. There we sat, across the table from each other, with matching gardenias and a bottle of fine red wine. I don't remember what we ate, but I do remember my sweet wife. I could tell that she was happy and content. The soft light in her eyes was reflected from the candles on the table. She smiled sweetly, and her lovely skin seemed to exude an aura of happiness. She was very beautiful. Our months apart had been long and difficult to endure.

The next day, we found a furnished room with a shared bathroom in a San Rafael private residence. It had a hot plate for cooking and a double bed with a broken spring, but it was the best we could find, and Nan said we'd make it do. We settled in. Back and forth I commuted from Hamilton Field to San Rafael, alternating army life and private life, living by the clock and early morning reveille.

One evening, I asked Nan to tell me about her new job at Woolworth's. "I'm behind the counter selling buttons and bows."

"That's a pretty swanky job, especially for a gal with a master's degree."

"It's not going to be a lifetime thing," she said, "but it will at least pay the rent on this crummy room, and it will give me something to do while you're away in the daytime."

"Hyde Street Trolley"

New men had been joining the 914th on a daily basis, and we were soon at full capacity. There was no proper space for us at crowded Hamilton, so they found a place up country for us. Oroville was a small town in the large open valley north of Sacramento. Scattered over the West Coast, the air force had set up emergency landing fields, places where a pilot in trouble could bring his plane down safely. Oroville was such a place, and they'd built some barracks there, the tar-paper kind near a dirt airstrip. So we formed a convoy and moved. I was almost sorry to leave Hamilton, for it had been a civilized place, a place with a good P.X. and a non-commissioned officers' club. At any rate, the convoy was all strung out on the road, the first time I'd ever seen our gear all in one place. There were several kinds of trucks: those used for hauling troops or supplies; those built for particular purposes, such as dragging big trailers; and those built like our modern-day campers, housing our presses, workrooms, darkrooms, and equipment having to do with mobile printing. Among the trucks were the usual couple of Jeeps for the officers, one of which was pulling our 37 Mil-field piece. It was very hot as we snaked through the traffic on the highway to our new home. Our job there was supposedly to maintain the airfield and to train as producers of maps and posters.

Our wives got together in San Rafael and came up on the bus. They scattered through Oroville and found places to live. Nan found a one-room furnished apartment over a two-car garage at a private residence. It was clean and airy and much better than the room in San Rafael. There, we had our own bathroom and decent facilities for cooking and eating. The bed in this place was okay, too—no broken springs!

It was hot in Oroville. I don't know which I liked least: the ice storms in Springfield, Missouri, where it would rain and freeze, icing up the trees and power lines until they dragged on the ground, with sidewalks and roads too slippery to walk or drive, or the heat in Oroville where an average day was 112 degrees and sometimes higher. Most days, we were out in it, doing close-order drill, fixing up the camp so it was habitable, or (preferably) lying in the shade when things were slack.

Our platoon sergeant was a street kid from New York—an Italian Jew. I don't remember his name because I made up my mind to forget this stupid honker as soon as possible. When he was given this job, he decided that HIS platoon was going to be the best goddamn platoon in the whole goddamn army. He took on the impossible. How can you make a spit-and-polish outfit out of a bunch of civilians who'd much rather be somewhere else? He tried hard, but we resisted his every move. One night he ordered us to clean the rough floor of the tar-paper barrack with our toothbrushes. This went on until some of the bigger fellows rebelled, ganged up on him, and suggested he mend his ways or else! It was better after that. I don't know whether it was the threat or the fires that did it. As I mentioned, it was unbearably hot there, so hot, in fact, that the whole country decided to burn itself up. I'm not sure if we were ordered by someone higher up or if we were just being neighborly, but we found ourselves with shovels and

"Expen-
sive
Date"

grubbing hoes out on the fire lines, trying to save homes and outbuildings from being consumed. The whole country seemed to be taken over by cheat grass that burned like crazy once it got started. The fire soon put an end to the spit and polish. It's hard to keep work boots shiny while working in smothering heat with a shovel.

Oroville seemed just as hot at night as it did in the daytime. Once when I was on guard duty, I was checking inside the barracks with my flashlight. I remember row after row of naked sweating bodies lying in their bunks. On nights like this at our place over the garage, the old swamp cooler would be cranking out temperatures not much cooler than the still night air around us.

Oroville was a place rife with orchards. Think of a square mile of plum trees. That would sure be a hell of a lot of plums when they all ripened at the same time in July. And a half-mile square of olive trees, not just one

"WARTIME ON MARKET STREET, SAN FRANCISCO"

orchard but two or three more just like it, was down the road. In addition, Oroville was home to citrus groves, one vineyard, and one small winery. Outside the window of our apartment stood a huge orange tree with a long reach over the yard. For breakfast, sometimes Nan would pick one luscious fruit right from the window without even going outside. They were so big, we'd split one. And Nan discovered a fig tree in the neighbor's yard and was invited to pick all she wanted by the friendly woman who owned the place. Nearer to town, right by the sidewalk, a kumquat tree bore sweet ripe fruit. Oroville was a friendly town. Everything there was to do happened at night, though. It was just too damned hot in the daytime.

"Vegetable Cart
in the Rain"

I was promoted to sergeant with three stripes on my sleeve. One day, I was given an assignment in "camouflage." I was supposed to disguise a truck so that from the air it would be recognized as something else. First off, I sent my truck and crew out to bring back a load of leafy shrubbery. While I waited, I sat and figured what I would do with it. Well, the truck came back and I looked it over. I was a sergeant now, so I knew all the words to use. "For Christ's sake!" I hollered. "You know what you brought me? A whole goddamn load of poison oak!" As an old farm boy and later a city Boy Scout, I knew poison oak when I saw it. "Take it out of here. Get rid of it. Burn it!" My gang did just exactly as I'd told them. They dumped their load right in the middle of the camp, poured gasoline on it, and set the whole thing on fire. It was green, so there was more smoke than fire, and the smoke filtered through the whole camp, carrying little globules of the poison. Then the whole goddamn camp wound up with one awful itch. I caught hell from the captain, and it took a case of GI soap and a little over a week before things settled back to normal again.

"Chinatown"

It was in Oroville that our gang took up hiking in earnest. First it was a two- or three-mile hike with our ten-pound M1 rifles. Then a five miler, and next a ten-mile hike in full field gear with rifles. The full field pack weighed close to thirty pounds. We worked our way up to a hike of twenty-six miles with rifle and full field gear. This was supposed to toughen us up. I was surprised, being only five-feet-eight-inches tall and probably the oldest in the group, that I could keep up with the younger kids. Every time, I was able to make it back on my own two feet. Some of the college boys, even the big football types, were occasionally brought home in the truck.

Oroville had more small black ants than I'd ever seen in one place at one time. One morning, a whole army of the little buggers crawled up the two stories of our outside wall, then underneath a loose-fitting window screen, down the inside wall, across the floor, and up the table leg to the sugar bowl on the table. A second line returned to the anthill with their loot. Nan solved this by spreading some sugar on the windowsill.

One pleasant aspect of our Oroville stay was the blooming magnolia tree in our front yard. One blossom alone would fill a large serving dish and make the whole house smell wonderful. Nan always did like flowers.

Just as we were settling in to our Oroville life, for some reason known only to army intelligence and our captain, we were ordered to move north to the town of Redding, California. The small airstrip and tar-paper barracks were very similar to those in Oroville, and it was just as hot and the grass fires just as plentiful. We hardly knew that we had moved, though Redding was larger with more and bigger buildings in its downtown area. Nan went house hunting with the other wives and found us a place in an old motel—one with a small

"Feeding Pigeons in the Park, San Francisco"

kitchenette. We had no orange trees or magnolias here, but Nan said she was happy. She found a job right off, folding sheets in a local laundry.

We were in Redding for the rest of the summer of 1943. Once we took our whole outfit on a trip: trucks, mobile printing facilities, the works, including a fair-sized gasoline generator to operate all the equipment. We took the winding mountain road up to Mt. Lawson, where we set up camp and slept in pup tents for two or three nights. Supposedly, we were a field outfit, and they wanted to see how we would operate in the field, using all of the specialized equipment. I don't know how we made out professionally, but it was interesting to see a volcanic mountain with a little steam still sputtering in its supposedly inactive bowels. Coming back down the mountain to Redding was something else, though.

The way the army chose its truck drivers was surely dreamed up by that same manic person who chose me for the medics because I'd had chemistry. The first prerequisite here was that the guy chosen should have an I.Q. of about 49; the next was that he wouldn't know a gearshift from a tailgate. Then the army turned him loose with the big four-by-four, the one with the same engine they use in the army M10 tanks. That's a wild combination and produces some very interesting situations when winding down a steep mountain. Most of the drivers in the 914th were fresh from the hat factories of New York, and they had never *ever* owned or driven any kind of a vehicle in their lives, so the ride down that mountain was a white-knuckled affair from top to bottom. Every time those big tires squealed on the winding turns, those of us riding in back who were pray-ers prayed, and those of us who were not shut our eyes and hoped we wouldn't end up in the gully of a mountain creek bottom. Twenty guys lying tangled and bloody in a smashed-up four-by-four was not a pretty picture. I had learned to drive in mountain country, and squealing tires in a big rig hauling twenty people bothered me a lot.

In 1943, Redding was a California boomtown. They were building Shasta Dam a few miles to the north, and the men who worked there were big spenders. Restaurants, bars, and other places of entertainment were really jumping. At that time, my sergeant's take-home pay-check was somewhere around forty dollars a month, with another forty dollars going to my wife as dependent, so a night on the town was almost prohibitive when paying the jacked-up prices charged the dam workers. We found a few places in town, though, where we could have a meal or listen to some music without spending an entire month's paycheck, and we made do with them. This was a lousy life compared to what we'd had pre-induction. It was especially hard on our women.

As the summer dragged on, the fires got progressively worse. It was a common experience to be sitting in a movie theater on a Sunday, relaxing and holding your wife's hand, when the lights would flicker, and big graphics would flash across the screen: "CAPTAIN PICKETT

WANTS YOU!" Outside would be one of our trucks, and we'd be hauled out to camp to change into our work clothes and pick up tools, then taken out to the fire line. They weren't our fires, but somehow we'd been assigned the dirty work. Once, north of town on a late afternoon, we had been directing our fire line so we could use the main highway as a fire stop. Some of our equipment was blocking traffic, and a bus carrying some dam workers back to town was stopped. Through the open windows, the workers started shouting at us, making catcalls and laughing. Our Captain Pickett was not amused. He walked to the bus, had the driver open the door, stuck his head inside and hollered, "I want you all to haul ass off this bus and line up outside, and by God make it fast!" They decided he wasn't joking and hauled ass out. "Now," he said, "You'll think this is a hell of a lot funnier after a couple of hours out here on the fire line. Get over there. Pick up some shovels. I'll show you where to start."

My next encounter with the dam workers took on a more personal touch. We'd been working all day on a particularly tough fire. The wind would pick up at the wrong time and wipe out hours of our work. It was getting late, and we were tired and hungry. Captain Pickett called to me, and when I stood before him, he unbuckled the forty-five caliber automatic pistol hanging at his waist. "Do you know how to use this, Sergeant?"

"Yes, Sir. Is it loaded?"

"Pickup on
Market Street"

"It's loaded. I want you to strap this on. Take a truck and a driver. I want you to bring me about twenty guys from town."

"What kind of guys, Sir?"

"Any kind that can use a shovel. We need help and I don't care where you get 'em. Just get 'em."

I got my truck and driver and headed for town. Now where in the hell was I going to get twenty guys? I started looking for populated places. Finally, I pulled up in front of a tough-looking bar on a side street near the middle of downtown. Here was a place of flowing beer and wild jukebox music. Most of the customers were sitting at the bar or at small tables lined up around the room. The first thing I did was head for the jukebox. I pulled the electric plug from its wall socket; the music stopped, and after an initial protest, everything got quiet. I pulled the holster of my forty-five around where everyone could see it. "I need twenty guys to help us fight a big fire. We're trying to keep some houses from burning, and we need you. When I pick you, I want you to go outside and get in the truck. Now, I want you, and you, and you. . . ." I think I was more surprised than they were when they did as they were told. I thought I'd get at least a little sass back, yet they went without a whimper.

"AT THE BAR"

"Street Sweeper"

Captain Pickett was very pleasant. "Did you have any trouble, Sergeant?"

"No, sir. I had to wrestle a few, but here's your twenty guys."

The whole summer was spent either fighting grass fires or hiking the less-traveled roads in the area. I remember the Feather River running almost through the town, and the orchards, and the view of the mountains to the east.

Along toward fall the 914th was on the move again, this time to Tacoma, Washington. Our gear, trucks, and all were loaded on a freight train. The night before we left, I was assigned to the railroad yards, guarding the train that stood on a side track ready to roll come morning. Guard duty at night is a lonesome, mind-deadening thing—blank, *nada*, nothing was happening—until the stillness was split wide open with the sounds of a motorcycle coming at least sixty miles per hour. Shattering the blackness, light came blazing down the paved road paralleling the tracks. I was a guard, right? So I stepped to the side of the road, held my rifle at a port-arms position and my chest high. I shouted, "HALT!" His tires lost a lot of rubber as he skidded past me, and I heard him yell, "You stupid son of a bitch!" So much for guard duty.

Foggy, soggy Tacoma—the few weeks I spent there were like a hazy dream. Most of the time the area was encased in an envelope of fog. Most things dripped. Those that didn't grew moss and mold. The 914th came up by train and the wives by bus. The first few days were a period of settling in. McChord Airbase, a few miles south of downtown Tacoma, was our new home. We were housed in two-story barracks, not as plush as those at O'Riley but nice and tight enough to keep out the fog. The second night there I met Nan, and we stayed in a tall hotel near the center of town. That night the air-raid sirens sounded, and we were told to pull the light-tight drapes on our windows and to turn off all unnecessary lights. This, to us, was a reminder that we were still at war. We had been in the outback all summer and had been so consumed with fighting grass fires that we had almost forgotten.

"Fisherman's Wharf"

Nan found a furnished room with bath and kitchen privileges. The room itself was okay, but Nan became very picky about the kitchen and eating arrangements when she found she was sharing her dishes with the family dog. "Oh, he's very clean. He's part of the family." Not to her, he wasn't!

I don't mind a little fog once in a while, but when you live in it, and have to come and go in it, it becomes a depressing thing. Objects in the distance are deeply hidden while close things loom up in ghostly forms. There are many tall evergreens on the streets of Tacoma. I felt surrounded by great silent shapes each time I ventured out. Nan hated the fog and said she felt "cooped up" with the combination of the small room and the gloomy outdoors, so in the evenings I walked with her and held her hand. We'd hear and feel the nearby traffic and footsteps of other walkers as they came near and passed us, but we couldn't see them. There was no escaping the fog once it closed in.

I was happy that the company had more or less given up on the long-hike program and had taken up map reading. They encouraged a long love affair with the M1 rifle too, and by the time we were through with the rifle course, we were able to take it apart, clean it, and put

"Heavy Date"

it back together again in the dark. They even let us shoot it once in a while. They'd load us up in trucks and take us down the road a few miles to the rifle range at Fort Lewis. This was pretty country when the fog would let you catch a glimpse of it. One day we were stretched out in various positions, banging away at our paper targets, when a small herd of white-tailed deer hesitantly came from a grove of tall pine trees and delicately picked their way between the shooters and our targets. "Hold your fire! Hold your fire!" shouted those in command, and the deer sauntered away, not even looking toward us as they disappeared into another grove of pines.

There were changes coming. Rumors were floating in the mess hall and latrine. The 914th was preparing to be shipped overseas. Overseas. What would it be like? Two wars were going on out there—one east, one west. Which one would we join? How long would we be gone? Would I be part of the percentage that wouldn't come back? We had more questions than answers.

A note on the bulletin board read: "Anyone interested in applying for OCS (Officer's Candidate School) please notify your C.O." I applied. I spent an hour before an examining board, passed their oral test, and was accepted. Either way—overseas or OCS—I knew my time with Nan would be brief.

Along with all the other wives, Nan was invited to attend our company mess hall for a Thanksgiving dinner that our cooks were preparing with turkey, pumpkin pie, and all the trimmings. She chose not to go, so we had a lonesome dinner in a small restaurant around the corner from our furnished room. We were the only customers at first, and the cooks made a great to-do over us, working hard to make everything special. Halfway through dinner another couple, African Americans, came in, and we finished our meal with them, departing the restaurant old friends.

Five of us were accepted by the board for OCS. The school was at Fort Belvoir in Virginia, across the Potomac from Washington, D.C. A class was starting in mid-December, and the 914th was leaving for overseas a couple of weeks earlier, so we were to be transferred to a sister outfit, the 915th, in Santa Rosa, California, while waiting. I kissed Nan good-bye and put her on a train for Salt Lake City. Our home had been rented so she would stay with her mother until things were back to normal. The next day, the five of us were on a train to Santa Rosa.

At the time I joined the 914th at Hamilton Field, I met Bob Lee, a Chinese American at least ten years younger than me and very much smarter. We were both civilians at heart, locked into a situation over which we had no control, and both trying hard not to make too many waves. We became close friends, and I was glad that he would be with me at OCS. Even today, I've kept track of him, and he's left his mark as a respected civil engineer. On the bus while riding into town, we heard tunes on the P.A. system from the musical *Oklahoma!* for the first time. Santa Rosa was another set of tar-paper barracks, and we weren't there long enough to get to know it well.

We rode the train cross-country to Virginia, Bob and I, first class all the way—linen and Lenox china, silver service, and Pullman porters. Why it wasn't all five of us traveling together, I don't recall, but it was just Bob and me.

"Bus Station"

We experienced a four-hour layover in Chicago with a four A.M. arrival and a cold wind whistling off the lake. Outside the station, it was well below zero, and we were both turning blue. We saw a USO at the end of the street and we hurried to it carrying our heavy duffel bags, wishing our long GI overcoats were fur lined. The sweet lady behind the counter gave us a cup of coffee and directed us to a cheap hotel two or three doors down the street. We checked in, climbed the stairs to our room, and found there was only one bed, but we were so cold that we piled in, overcoats, boots, and all. It was good to get warm again.

Fort Belvoir was the hub-point of everything to do with the Engineering Service of the U.S. Army. It's near Alexandria, Virginia, and sits at the edge of a great hardwood forest. At the time I was there, it was a place of rotating classes for the purpose of making officers (and gentlemen) out of ordinary GIs. There were many buildings, but I was acquainted only with the two-story barrack where I was assigned, the mess hall, and four or five different classrooms. Lee and I were with a platoon-sized group of about thirty men. There were three platoons to a company, and the company was considered a class. The course was to last twenty-one weeks. With three companies moving through the system, we had enough men to form a battalion.

One class was several weeks ahead of us, and another several weeks ahead of them. Everything I'd ever heard about West Point applied to the classes going through Belvoir. Although the candidates varied in rank from private to master sergeant, we were all treated equally like the freshmen we were. We were supposed to run everywhere we went, and there was a place between the barracks and the mess hall called the "bar," which was a length of two-inch pipe anchored between two posts. Every time we passed this place, we were supposed to do twenty-five chin-ups. At reveille we were given just so many minutes to visit the latrine, make our beds, and appear for roll call and calisthenics before running to the mess hall and then running to a day of classes.

"Bring Us Two More"

Here is a sampling of things I learned at OCS: how to build a pontoon bridge across a river (in winter); how to fire and maintain every weapon issued to the army (pistols, rifles, grenade launchers, machine guns [thirty and fifty caliber], field pieces such as the thirty-five and seventy-five millimeter [both stationary and on wheels], and bazookas); how to throw a hand grenade; how to not only find a buried land mine but to disable it; and how to blow up a bridge or a house or anything that needed blowing up. We also learned to drive every kind of vehicle issued to the engineers, such as jeeps, trucks, big trucks, road graders, and bulldozers. And, last but not least, we were taught how to plan the trajectory, fire, and blow up a dummy tank a half mile away with a seventy-five-millimeter field piece. At the time, I could perform any of these tasks, but I'd hate to be asked to start and drive a bulldozer now.

Hand-to-hand combat was also emphasized. I learned how to kill a man coming at me with his own knife, how to throw a two-hundred-pound man over my shoulder, and how to play touch football on a gravel parking lot ("And if I catch you playing TOUCH football, I'll flunk the whole bunch," an instructor told us).

We made several night hikes in the snow where what sleep we had was with only a blanket. We also did nighttime map hikes. Divided into parties of three, we were given a map, a compass, and a small flashlight. We were at point A, and we were to make our way through the thick forest to point B, which was two miles on the other side of the forest, then report back to point A. The weather was cold and the snow was halfway to our knees. As we tramped through the ghostly trees we were constantly worried that we were lost.

We ran our own company. Each day on the bulletin board there was a list designating an acting captain, lieutenant, officer of the day, and various sergeants. These extra duties were in addition to the activities and classes. Every couple of weeks there was a parade where we would pass in review with flags flying and the post band playing Sousa marches. This whole thing was spit and polish and, I thought, matched anything West Point could have mustered.

Most of my memories of Belvoir concern the constant running, the pressure of never having enough time to do what was required. I remember the three-minute fifty-cent haircuts, the inspections when the officers bounced coins on our bunks to see if the blankets were tight, the two-mile runs with full field gear, pack, and rifle, and the hike on the other side of the forest where we passed by Mt. Vernon. Everything at Belvoir was directed toward the lean and mean.

Some Sundays we were allowed to go into Washington, D.C. Lee and I visited the Smithsonian Institute, the various monuments, and strolled past the White House. When I was a civilian artist, I had a written invitation to visit the grand opening of the National Museum of Art. Now I finally got to see it and enjoyed the exhibit and the new building. Also, when I was a civilian and head of Utah's Federal Arts Program, Washington sent a writer, Darell

McConkey, to Utah to help out with the publication of a guidebook by the Writer's Project. The McConkeys lived in a suburb west of Washington, and when I made my presence known to them, they invited me to spend Christmas Day with them and have dinner. I asked if I could bring a friend. They were happy to include him, so I took Lee with me.

We enjoyed a delicious dinner and a friendly feeling. Afterward, I asked Darell if I could use his phone to call my wife. I wished her and all the family at home a merry Christmas, told her how sorry I was not to be with her, and also sorry that I hadn't sent some kind of present.

"That's okay," she said. "I've got one for you, though; I'm pregnant!"

I was stunned for a moment, then I asked, "Are you happy about it?"

"I couldn't be happier," she said.

"Then I'm happy, too."

We couldn't have picked a lousier, more mixed-up time for this to happen, but I thought, what the hell? Things couldn't be any more mixed-up than they already were.

It was going well for me at OCS. My marks were high, and I found out I could keep up with my peers physically, even though they were young college types. After all the pull-ups, push-ups, and sit-ups, I felt strong and lusty like in my freshman year at college after spending the prior summer jockeying a jackhammer on a construction job. Just two more weeks and it would all be over.

The first week in April, I was called into the C.O.'s office. "I have bad news for you, Sergeant Bird," said the captain. "How old are you?"

"Just this week turned thirty-three, Sir," I answered.

"We're sorry, Sergeant, but the engineers are not accepting anymore thirty-three-year-old Second Lieutenants. Had you been in the class preceding this one, you would have been accepted. Your grades were okay, but the law was effective April first."

I was very upset. Almost shouted at him, "What a lousy deal! You let me go through all this for nineteen weeks, let me get measured for an officer's uniform, and now you tell me?" Instead, I said, "What am I supposed to do now?"

"Go pack your gear, everything except your rifle. You'll be transferred to another barrack, a holding company, until we figure out what to do with you."

Well, p—s on the whole goddamned army! It was more tar-paper barracks, and the first thing I asked for was a weekend pass. I got on a train to New York City, thinking I might as well see some of the sights while I was there. I had three days and two nights.

During the war years, New York was a "serviceman's town." There were no big army or navy bases nearby, and those few visitors in uniform were given the red-carpet treatment. I registered at a hotel near Fifth Avenue and Forty-second Street. "Yes, sir. We reserve a few good

"NEWSPAPER
MAN ON
CORNER"

rooms for our service people. That will be $4.00 for the night, and if you are interested in see-ing a show tonight, here is a ticket to *Carmen Jones*. It's on the house."

It was a wonderful show. The next day I set out to see the city. When boarding the two-decker London-style bus, the motorman put his hand over the fare box. "You guys in uniform ride free. Enjoy the ride."

I had been on the run for nineteen weeks at Belvoir. Now I sauntered around New York, taking in the city sights. I strolled over to Central Park, then to the Museum of Modern Art. Here my old Art Project boss, Holgar Cahill, and his wife, Dorothy Miller, were on the staff. They were surprised to see me and made me welcome, then invited me to their apartment down in the Colony for a steak dinner that evening.

Back in the tar-paper barrack at Belvoir, I was bored and felt like a ham being smoked by the potbellied coal stove. I went to the office to inquire if any decision had been made toward my future, and when the C.O. said no, I asked him if he'd get me some art materials. I would do a mural in their dayroom. Anyway, this was something to do.

I started work on a relatively clear wall opposite the door. My subject was a comic look at army life, singling out things like KP and the long hikes. I had it all drawn out, first in char-coal, then blocked out in color with oils. Then the call came, and it was never finished.

"We're trying to find an outfit where you'd fit in, Sergeant. You were in the air force, right?"

"An engineering outfit attached to the air force, Sir."

"Well, those of you in the air force have some choice in where you will be sent."

The army had dealt me a low blow; now it was my turn. "I'd like to be sent back to my old outfit the 915th Air Force Headquarters Company in Santa Rosa, California." I knew that the 915th had been disbanded and no longer existed. Maybe in all the mix up, I could some-how better myself.

Soon I was on a train for San Francisco with a bus ticket up to Santa Rosa, and a three-day layover in Salt Lake City. I found my sweet Nan very pregnant. We held hands during my brief stay and decided to name our baby Robyn May. "We'll call her Robyn."

"How do you know it will be a girl?" I asked.

"I just know," she said.

"At the Corner,
Fisherman's Wharf
San Francisco"

The Fourth Air Force Headquarters was at Montgomery and Mission Street in downtown
San Francisco. When I reported in with my orders for the old 915th, they seemed much surprised and confused. They hadn't the slightest idea what to do with me, so I was sent to their
barrack, given a bed, shown to the mess hall, and told to report back at headquarters each day.
The barrack was really something. They had taken an office building at Fourth, near Market
Street. It was remodeled to make a big mess hall out of the lobby, a great lounge and dayroom
from a big chunk of the top floor, deluxe latrines from the old expanded restrooms that includ-
ed toilet stalls, and bunkrooms from the offices. I was in a small room with two other guys,
and I had a locker and a mattress on a cot with springs.

    For several days, I was in and out of headquarters, and in my wanderings, I found
myself visiting their drafting room, which was presided over by a Warrant Officer with engineering buttons on his collar. We talked. I told him my story, said I was an artist and had some
high-school drafting. Could he use me in his department? He could and we went to the proper

people, so I became a Sergeant Technician in the Drafting Department of Fourth Air Force Headquarters. If I had to be a soldier, this was the best duty I could possibly find. I kept my bunk in the office/barrack, enjoyed the excellent food in the mess hall, and had a nine-to-five job five days a week with a permanent pass that permitted me to wander anyplace within reason during my free hours.

The drafting room was filled with maps, very large roll-down maps, hanging from the walls. They were maps of all the airfields under 4th Air Force command, including landing fields like Oroville and Redding. Our job was to keep them current. Any changes made, such as new buildings, extended runways, or others, were so noted and the maps were changed accordingly. It was one of the most cushy jobs I've ever had before or since.

"Shipyard Workers Swing Shift"

I was no stranger to San Francisco. It was only a day and a half drive from Salt Lake, and Nan and I had made the trip on several occasions. We had also sometimes taken the forty-minute bus trip to the big city while we were stationed in San Rafael. On most of these excursions, we had visited my brother Joe and his wife Hazel. Joe was semiretired and owned a small mom-and-pop grocery store in the northwest outskirts of the city. He had a nice apartment out near the small boat harbor.

Even though I had a great job and swank army living conditions, my take-home pay was still only $42.00 per month, and this was poor pickings in San Francisco with its more highly paid local shipyard workers and sailors on leave. I found I could blow my whole forty-two bucks in one evening if I wasn't careful. So on Saturdays I worked at my brother's store, stocking his shelves and bagging groceries for him when he was busy. Occasionally he would take me home with him, where Hazel would have dinner waiting, and he would break out a bottle of good Napa Valley wine.

After graduating from OCS and becoming a second lieutenant, my friend Bob Lee was sent to San Francisco to learn Cantonese. The army obviously had in mind some special assignment for him. We got together in the evenings, sometimes for dinner and sometimes for a walk around town. Once he took me on an underground tour of Chinatown through a maze of dark tunnels beneath the streets and buildings.

When we had left Tacoma, I sent my 1943 Midwest sketches home with Nan. She showed them to Charlie Pittenger, my old friend at Intermountain Art Company. He liked them well enough to cut mats for them and promote an exhibition at the University of Utah's Union Building. Because of our hectic life in California, Washington, and Belvoir, I hadn't touched my sketchbooks, but now I was sketching again. I couldn't resist drawing some things on my long walks through Golden Gate Park, along the beach, and prowling the streets and back alleys of the city. Sometimes I'd take my sketchbook with me and make rough pencil sketches. Then in the evenings in the dayroom, I'd work them over in ink. Or I'd draw what I'd seen from memory.

All this time, I'd been worried about Nan and was in constant touch with her by phone and letter. She'd been hospitalized. The pregnancy wasn't going well. The doctors decided to operate and a cesarean was performed early in the eighth month. Afterward she called me from the hospital. She hadn't fully recovered from the anesthesia and sounded groggy. "Don't come home now. I'm such a mess. The baby is a girl. I've seen her once, but they're keeping her in an incubator." She was sobbing. "I don't know for how long. I don't want you to see us like this. Wait until I bring her home. I love you. Please wait. I love you." Our Robyn was born on May 20, 1944.

That evening I called her mother's house, and we talked about my new daughter—how much she weighed, how much hair she had, and all the rest. I told Nan's cousin Betty, who was living there then and studying to be a nurse, to go buy a single red rose for Nan, and I'd send her the money. That's all I could think of doing at the time. All I could do was worry and wait.

I didn't see my new daughter until she was almost a month old. She looked like all babies do when newborn, except this one was very small, with a lot of dark hair, and was very special to me. I'd managed a week for the trip, but most of it was used up with riding the bus each way. Then I was back on the coast again, back to the drawing board.

I hate name-droppers when they dig up important people they've met or known and parade them before me in almost every conversation. I usually stop them with, "I've rubbed elbows with Hap Arnold." He was a four-star general in charge of the U.S. Army Air Force, just under General Marshal, Chief of Staff. Anyway, I did almost rub elbows with him; only a wall-mounted metal partition was between us when we used adjoining urinals in Fourth Air Force Headquarters' restroom. And there was a day when I was working in the drafting room through the noon hour, doing some catch-up work, when he wandered in and talked with me, just the two of us, for maybe half an hour. I thought he was an okay guy. He didn't talk down to me in any way.

A similar incident happened a couple of weeks later. This time it was a major, a medium-sized, light-complexioned guy. He said he'd been an architect in civilian life, and we were talking a little about architects when I got up enough nerve to say, "I'd like to meet the horse's ass architect who designed the tar-paper barracks. He sure screwed up when he did that one."

"I'm Major Stone," he said. "I'm the horse's ass who did it," and he walked out.

At this time, San Francisco was barely coping with all the action taking place within its borders. It was literally bursting at the seams. The downtown area would sometimes come to a standstill, clogged with workers from the nearby shipyards and munitions plants, with cable and trolley cars, trucks and automobiles, all making their own peculiar racket. I'm certain that half of all our military forces on leave or on duty were packed and jammed on the sidewalks, streets, parks, strip joints, and bars. I could look down from the windows of our dayroom on the fifth floor and see almost solid white hats of our on-leave navy moving along Market Street. Like a projection of blood cells in the veins and arteries of an arm, each cell joining a moving stream, coming or going, pushing to a final destination, all with much noise and confusion.

To me, it was all exciting: Fishermen's Wharf, Chinatown, Market Street, the harbor, the beaches, Golden Gate Park, the old decaying area of the

"Shoe Shine Boys at Work"

Embarcadero. Add to this the wild mix of people, plus the sights, sounds, and smells of a city very much alive; whether it be enveloped in rain, in fog, or in sunshine, to me San Francisco was, and still is, a very special place.

In September, it was good-bye to the plush city-living by the bay. The army didn't tell its buck sergeants any of its strategic moves beforehand, but I found out later that after retaking the Philippines, they were about to try ending the war by readying an invasion of the Japanese homeland islands. In my case it was "last ones here, first to go."

I was sent to Geiger Field near Spokane, Washington, where the 1903rd Engineer Aviation Battalion was being formed. It was a heavy-equipment outfit, prepared to build airfields, roads, and other needed structures. The city of Spokane was a quiet place after San Francisco, set in lush green country with lots of evergreen trees. In September, the leaves on the leafy trees and underbrush were starting to show fall colors.

"Fishing off the Wharf"

New men were coming every day from everywhere, and it was a question, at first, where each man would fit in. The battalion consisted of about five hundred and twenty-five officers and men, making up Headquarters and A, B, and C Companies. I was assigned to C Company under command of Captain Herbert Schiff. We underwent a basic training period and some confusion, but in a few weeks things began to come together.

Geiger Field was in an area to the west of town. The barracks we were assigned were the two-story, comfortable kind, with mess halls and company offices and dayrooms. I found out early on that married men could live off base, and I found a tract place the city had built for war-industry people working in the area. They were very small units with living/dining/kitchen in an open area and a closed-off bath and one bedroom. Fairly new and clean, they were heated by wood-burning stoves. Dry wood was cut and piled in the street, and every unit could take what it needed; each unit was provided with an ax for cutting. Nan and our new little Robyn came from Salt Lake City by train. We were a family again.

Back in June when I'd first seen my daughter, she was a tiny squirming thing that fit nicely in one hand and forearm. Now she was a small, ever-moving, inquisitive bundle of button nose, big eyes, and ever-exploring hands. Nan was a great mother, and she'd done well by our Robyn, who was a sweet and healthy child. The time I had to spend with them was a happy time of shared love for each other.

The days at Geiger Field were a bustle of preparation and training. I was assigned to a camouflage unit where we covered some of our equipment with netting and pieces of brush from the nearby forest. Then it was arranged for us to view the installation from the air. We boarded an army-reject plane that reminded me of the Dog Patch plane in *Lil' Abner*, complete with floppy wings and a few prominent patches. And if the plane wasn't bad enough, the pilot who came with it was a long lean Texas cowboy whose only object in life was "raisin' hell and havin' fun." This was my first time in an airplane, and I'll never forget it. To begin with, it was not a plane for comfortably viewing anything. There was one small peek-hole window on both sides and a front-end nose of Plexiglass. The plane had a seat up front for one person and a spot under the seat if I lay on my belly flat out on the glass. This was the place they put me. It was as if I was floating with nothing under me but air, and it was a white-knuckled sensation when our crazy cowboy decided to buzz a tower at a small field we passed. It was not one of my better days.

I also recollect a memorable field trip. We had all our heavy equipment loaded up, and we were traveling spread out on the road, heading for a place in the rolling hills above Yakima. There, we were to see if we could build an airstrip. Our camp was made up mostly of six-men tents. They were new, square, and suspended from a tall center pole. Along the side of the pole

was a metal chimney from a small wood-burning stove. It was late fall and cold out, so the fellows promptly got their stoves going with truck-supplied coal. We were to learn that the waterproofing on the tents was not fireproof. The first night alone, five tents burned to the ground, leaving in each case six surprised guys shivering in their cots.

I was given a truck and a driver to go into town for coal. The driver and I had to shovel it off a railroad car onto the truck, and by the time we got back to camp, it was dark. I stopped in the mess tent for a snack and to pick up a five-gallon can of water for our tent. No one told me they'd dug a four-foot-deep garbage pit just off the back door of the tent, and I stepped off into it, carrying the heavy water can. I came out of there covered with garbage, with a sprained knee, and using all the cuss words I'd ever known to describe the stupid cooks, including, often and creatively, the "f" word.

We had found a fairly flat place on the mountain to build our airstrip. The cold was bitter up there, and to make matters worse, it had snowed enough to make it muddy. My job, now that I was limping with a bad knee, was to direct the trucks hauling dirt and gravel as to where they should dump their loads so that the bulldozers could spread it and compact it. I was assigned a surveyor's level and a rod man so I could tell the low and high spots.

This was my second Thanksgiving in the army. I remember squatting on the ground, staring at my mess kit. We were given turkey, mashed potatoes, gravy, sweet potatoes, cranberry sauce, and green salad, all piled up together and topped with a huge scoop of vanilla ice cream. I hoped Nan and Robyn were faring better than I.

"Southern Boy"

Shortly after returning to Geiger Field, I was called to Captain Schiff's office. I was asked if I would serve as his first sergeant. "There are some strings attached," he said. "You would have to serve as a three-stripe sergeant until there's an opening for further promotion." The battalion only allowed a certain number of those with six stripes and the allotment was full. "You'll get promoted as openings occur." This was unexpected on my part, but I accepted and was now the new first sergeant of Company C.

Things changed for me dramatically. First, I'd been told by those over me what to do and when and where I could do it. Now I was doing the telling. First thing every morning my company clerk and I prepared a Daily Morning Report, stating how many of the one hundred and twenty-five guys in the company were there and on the job, and who was absent and why. I had a duty roster showing where every one of the one hundred and twenty-five were at any given time. I could issue a pass or toss some private on KP for an infraction. I took orders only from the captain. Other than that, I was the "Head Rooster."

I soon found out that my main job was dealing with people. I'm sure in forming our outfit that the army knew exactly what it was doing. If they had some guy whose purpose was unclear, they'd send him up to the 1302nd at Geiger Field. Somehow in all the confusion we got some good people and also some rotten apples. I'd say that 85 to 90 percent of my guys were okay, always on time and making no waves, but we also had some real characters.

One of the better soldiers, "Big Money" we called him, came from somewhere in the South. He was six-foot-three and two ax handles wide across the shoulders. He had me read his mail and write letters home for him. Big Money laughed often and would do anything asked of him.

Another good man, Sergeant Hunt, was one of the best supply sergeants in the army. No matter what we needed, he'd get it for us. Hard-to-get items were traded or scrounged for, but we got them.

One of the stranger men, Private "John H," was a guy who wouldn't take a bath. Some of his roommates complained to me. "Give him a bath, then," I said. So six men grabbed him one night and scrubbed him down with GI soap and a floor brush.

"What did you do, John, before you were in the army?"

"I was a butter," he told me.

"What's a butter?"

"A butter is like this." He ran really fast and smashed his head against the tailgate of a four-by-four truck.

"Do you get much work, John?"

"Well, when the carnival comes, I keep real busy."

As near as I ever found out, "John H" had no further accomplishments.

Private Fargnoli was a tailor. In all his life he'd done nothing but tailoring. He screwed up everything he was asked to do, even KP. What the hell do you do with a tailor? It took me a while, but later on I was able to use his talent.

Private Brinton was a tough guy from Shreveport, Louisiana. "I ain't takin' no sh-t from nobody. Not from you, not from the captain, not from nobody else in the whole f—-ing army!" What could I do with a guy like that?

Another of the bad apples, Sergeant Bagly, was a born gambler. This kid always had a game going in our dayroom, sometimes several at the same time. Often, the fellow who wanted to read or listen to the radio could not get near the place because Bagly had it full of gamblers. They came most every evening from all over Geiger Field. After complaints, I hauled him in to see the captain. Suppose we kicked him out of the dayroom? He'd just go someplace else, and he said so. "But I'll tell you what I'll do," he continued. "I'll give you a percentage if you'll let me stay."

So we agreed. Then he really had the dayroom hopping. Besides poker tables, he set up a craps shooting area and a rickety roulette wheel that he'd dug up somewhere. Before we left the States, we had a sizeable chunk of money that we invested in some goodies that weren't supplied by the army, such as refrigeration equipment, metal screens, toilet paper, and razor blades.

Of the characters I encountered, these were the most memorable of the 1302nd of Geiger Field.

Back on the home front, the holidays were creeping up on us. This would be Robyn's first Christmas, and our time together was slipping away. Both Nan and I set out to make it one we'd not soon forget. I took the ax from the wood box and went deep into the surrounding forest where I found a tall fir tree that looked promising, climbed it, and hacked off the top. Trimming the tree without ornaments was simple. We took a roll of aluminum foil and a pack of hairpins and made crude bells, tubes, and balls. Then we strung some cranberries and pop-corn. It wasn't as fancy as what we were used to, but I'll always remember it. And our Robyn liked it so much that it ended up in her playpen to keep her from tearing it apart. I wondered how Nan managed such a great dinner on the wood-burning stove, and, making it even more festive, Nan's uncle's wife's brother, Jack Baker, who was stationed at a nearby naval base, joined us. It was a great Christmas.

Our last days together went by very fast, and it was a sad time late in January 1945 when I put my two gals on the train for Salt Lake City. There was much hugging, kissing, and flowing tears; even little Robyn was crying. By the middle of February, our whole battalion was on another train with all our gear and heavy equipment headed for Seattle and Fort Lawton.

E.J.BIRD

"Give Me a Six"

Fort Lawton was on Seattle's waterfront, a place made up of barracks, warehouses, and assorted buildings all geared to processing ships, troops, and supplies to and from the far reaches of the Pacific. In the short time we were there, we got shots in both arms and rump and had the so-called final physical that featured over five hundred naked men all at one time and in one building. One night three or four of us went into town to see a show. When we got back to the gate, the guards there were beating up some drunken skinny kid. They were really working him over. I'd never seen the kid before, but I hated what I was seeing, so I spoke up. "He's one of mine. I'll take care of him." So we took the kid, half dragging him into the main part of the base. Somehow he got loose, took a wild swing, and caught me alongside my jaw and knocked me down. We tossed him into the first barrack we came to, and that's the last we ever heard about it.

During this time, Private Brinton went AWOL, and we hoped they'd never catch him before we left. It would be one way to be rid of him and the future problems he was sure to bring us, but we had bad luck and the MPs delivered him to us the night before we left. Next day, he was placed in the ship's brig. We turned him loose when we hit the high seas.

"Prawns
and Fresh
Crab"

Diary February 6

Well, here we go. Got everything but a return ticket—full pack, gas mask, steel helmet, and combat boots that still hurt from their newness. We pile out of the trucks and line up in the mist. I'm the first man aboard number one the First Sergeant. God damn! I even get a guide to show me to my quarters!

It's a relief to shed the pack—had it too damn tight across the shoulders. So, this is the LST 840. Twelve men in our compartment, three deep in canvas bunks. There are no mattresses, but we have a small locker. Six GIs with six Navy. Hope we get along. No smoking the smoking lamp is out. Wish I had a cigarette.

I remembered what Capt. Tupper had said. "Those LSTs are okay, but they're flat bottomed, and they get pushed around, see. They rock sideways and don't cut the water, and when she rears up, she comes down like this, see, and quivers all over like a new bride."

We must be moving—the deck is. I can't get seasick. I'll go see. I just heard a whistle someplace. Better take a last look at things, or am I sentimental? It's a lot different feeling than when you buy your own ticket. That way you always come back if you want to. Nan doesn't know I'm on my way today, but she will when she stops getting my letters. What a God damned life!

I'm okay as long as I lie down and don't eat much. Take Allen here down on his knees, hugging the pot. Oh, oh! I'm going to have to join him.

Ship's Log
The Good Ship LST 840

Left Seattle, Washington	6 Feb 45
Arrived Pearl Harbor (T.H.)	9 Mar 45
Left Pearl Harbor	13 Mar 45
Arrived Eniwetok	24 Mar 45
Left Eniwetok	24 Mar 45
Arrived Guam	29 Mar 45
Left Guam	30 Mar 45
Arrived Ulithe	1 Apr 45
Left Ulithe	12 Apr 45
Arrived Nago Wan (Okinawa)	18 Apr 45
Left Nago Wan	20 Apr 45
Arrived IE Shima (Okinawa)	20 Apr 45

"Lighting Up"

It took three of these LST flat-bottomed ships to contain all our heavy equipment. Trucks, bulldozers, graders, rollers, shovels, and other equipment were chained to the lower covered decks so they wouldn't shift in a heavy sea. The whole front of the ship converted into a ramp for loading and unloading. On the top exposed flat deck, each ship carried an LCI (landing craft infantry), and chained to both sides of every ship was a four-by-four, seventy-five-foot-long pontoon made of quarter-inch steel plate to be used somewhere in the future for a dock. Each of the LCIs built to haul maybe thirty-five men had an open deck now filled with army cots to carry our overflow, all covered with a huge canvas top to keep out the weather. A, B, and C Companies were each assigned to an LST, and Headquarters Company was divided between us, so that meant each of the three ships carried maybe one hundred seventy army men along with the regular navy personnel.

With all our gear in chained-down boxes, the LCI and various other items scattered about, this did not make for luxurious sea travel. Around the perimeter and at the lower-deck level of the LSTs was a corridor eight or nine feet wide. This was our living quarters, with built-in bunks and latrines, ship's gear, and lockers. The bunks were on the outside wall of the corridor. So with the ship rocking from side to side, the heavy pontoons would swing out, then back, smashing into the ship's metal side with a resounding crash not more than a foot away from where we were sleeping.

I will say this for the navy: their food, in spite of serving beans for breakfast every Wednesday, was much better than anything I'd had in the army, and their coffeepot was going twenty-four hours a day.

After I finally got my sea legs, I had no trouble with being seasick, but it seemed to take forever to get anywhere on the slow plodding LSTs. With no particular duties to occupy us, the gamblers took over, and, as expected, our Sergeant Bagly had all the gambling money at journey's end. CONTINUED ON PAGE 97

"IE Shima Beachouse"
 above and
"Untitled," left

Previous Spread:
"The Well, Okinawa",
This Page:
"The War - It's hard on Everyone"
Following Spread:
"IE Shima, The War's Been Here"

E.J. BIRD

E J BIRD

E. J. Bird

Okinawa "Old Man" and "Fishing Boat," opposite.

"Small Fry" Opposite (clockwise from upper left:) "Fancy Pants"; "They Carry Heavy Loads"; "Okinawa Dispossessed"; "They Carry It If They Can Lift It"

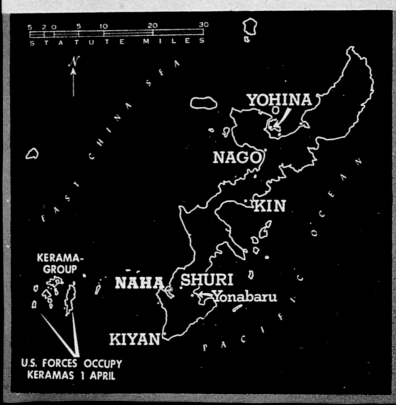

OKINAWA

5 0   5   10   20   30
S T A T U T E   M I L E S

N

EAST CHINA SEA

YOHINA

NAGO

KIN

KERAMA-
GROUP

NAHA   SHURI
Yonabaru

KIYAN

PACIFIC   OCEAN

U.S. FORCES OCCUPY
KERAMAS 1 APRIL

APRIL 1
HUN
SEE THE
MORNIN
FLASHES
OCCASION
AND ON
MEN DU
LIGHTER
AND SOM
SEEMED
TOWARD
AND OUR
OUT OF
SEE THE
SMOKE A
POUND O
ENOUGH
LEAST M
GLIDED
THE SOO
PLANES
YOU COU
OUR NA
B
ANCORA
VERY CL
WE WER

When we left the States, we had no idea of the vastness of the Pacific Ocean. It seemed to go on forever. The day before we reached the Hawaiian Islands, where our three ships would be tied up side by side in Pearl Harbor in view of our wrecked and sunken ships from Japan's initial attack, we slapped Private Brinton into the ship's brig for safekeeping. Later, while walking down a crowded Honolulu street on shore leave, I was surprised to see him coming toward me with two of his navy buddies. They had him dressed in a sailor's uniform! When we passed, I merely smiled and waved to him. He waved back.

We passed Johnson's Island, Eniwetok, tied up in Guam for half a day (no one got ashore except some of the naval personnel), and sailed on to Ulithe. Ulithe was a group of very small islands set around a huge, deep lagoon where hundreds of our ships were at anchor. Ulithe is part of the Carolinas. We were told that they were formed by a huge volcano, and the islands that we see are the exposed pieces of the rim. Each island was an acre or two of sand and palm trees, beautiful and very hot.

One of the islands, Mog Mog, was set aside for R and R. Each day while we were anchored there, a small boat would come by and take those of us who wanted to stretch our legs to shore. Here the navy had set up a generator that operated a huge walk-in refrigerator full of beer and Coke. We were allowed to buy one beer or two Cokes per trip.

One of the things that they had installed for having fun was a boxing ring. On this particular day, the marines had taken it over and were offering ten bucks for anyone who could beat their fighter. While we were tied up in Pearl Harbor, I had seen one of my guys, a Hopi Indian from Arizona, work over a couple of fighters A and B Companies had produced, and I liked his style, so I challenged the marines. My Indian weighed only half as much as the big marine, yet completely outfought him. I walked off with the ten bucks, half of which I shared with him. I found out later that he had fought as a pro in Arizona.

They had moved all the natives off the little island, yet one day I saw a strange sight. A little old man in nothing but a breach cloth was harvesting coconuts. He'd shinny up the tall tree, twist off the nuts, and toss them to the ground. After gathering the nuts about him, he sat down and with his two bare feet reached for a coconut, maneuvered it around to suit him, and whacked off the husks with a huge machete, just missing his bare toes. I wondered how he had any toes or feet left to work with.

The purpose of anchoring at Ulithe was to be part of a convoy of ships bound for Okinawa. When we headed north, we were in the center of maybe a dozen others. We were not well armed, and we made slow progress in relation to the warships that were protecting us. Destroyers were whipping around our perimeter like playful puppies, searching for floating mines that were seen at times in this part of the ocean. According to my ship's log, we were six days away from Okinawa.

Diary April 18

Hunt dragged me out of bed at 0400 to see the activity on shore. In the early morning darkness we could see the flashes and hear the pounding of guns. Occasionally a flare shell would burst and one could imagine the scurry of men ducking for cover. As it grew lighter the various islands stood out, and someone pointed out Okinawa. There seemed to be a great commotion in toward shore on the southwest tip, and our warships were shelling hell out of something or other. We could see the flash and rise of powder smoke, and way later could hear the pounding of the guns. We seemed safe enough with our Destroyer escort. At least nobody seemed worried, and we glided up the coast, wondering what the score was. There were lots of planes about, and everywhere you looked you could see the fighting ships of our navy.

By noon we were at our anchorage and could see the shore very clearly through the glasses. We were in a small bay surrounded by rolling hills. Near the center and extending around the beach and fingering up the valleys was a small village of sorts. The maps called it Nago. It looked badly beat up around the shoreline, and there were a few disconsolate black cows exploring the debris just beyond the water's edge. Rising up behind the town's buildings were the colorful terraced garden patches, and the wind-shaped pines so common in all the photos of the Orient. All the buildings looked as if they were made of rock or adobe, with roofs of gray tile or thatched with straw. Under other conditions the place would have been a very peaceful farming center, but now with GI vehicles kicking up a dust on the road just behind the sea wall it was anything but that.

All kinds of landing craft were disgorging tanks on the beach, and an aid station in the form of a fly tent was set up nearby. On a point to our right an artillery unit was banging away at something, and a light cruiser just off our bow was blasting at the hill behind the town. It would be interesting to know what was going on and not try to correlate what we were seeing with our own eyes while listening to Radio Tokyo. At least we knew it was not maneuvers!

Diary April 19, Nago Wan

Here we sit in the bay, wondering what all the shooting's about. We've been examining the shore through the glasses, watching the shore battery bang away, but can't see what they're hitting. Occasionally the cruiser opens up and we see smoke rising behind the hill. Last night we watched the star shells and could see flashes to the north.

Heard on the radio this morning about Ernie Pyle. Shot through the forehead by a Jap machine gun on IE Shima. Just found out that's where we're headed. It's ten or fifteen miles from here, a very small island on the north spur of this bay. We could see them shelling and bombing the hell out of it when we came in yesterday. There's a volcanic-like mountain on the east end of

it, which makes it easy to identify. The marines and infantry landed there yesterday. Too bad about Pyle. He was a favorite of the GIs everywhere.

They must be burning the houses in the village. Once in a while a thatched roof will go up in flames and there's been no shooting in that section.

Diary April 20

Somebody said we'll hit the island tonight, but the biggest news is mail call. First letters from home in thirty-seven days. God damn! Letters from Nan—seven of them, and pictures of Robyn. Must be more mail someplace. Everybody's happy and sentimental. It's hazy and cold, and all our warm clothes are in our duffel bags.

Mid-afternoon now and we're headed out of the bay. We'll see what IE looks like up close.

There it is, the one with the hump on it. Warships are laying in toward the southwest tip and explosions are taking place at the base of the mountain. Our new home looks far from peaceful. Jesus! Are they bombing the boats? A huge jet of water is rising like Old Faithful. It could be almost anything through all the smoke, it's hard to tell. Just passed a wrecked ship. Gives you a funny feeling to see her lying there, so newly killed. We're close now. You can feel the concussion of the big guns. Looks like they're concentrating all their fire on the base of the mountain and there's a plane flying round and round like a hawk. It's dark before we notice, and there's a full moon shining bright above us, and we're watching the fifties send their burning tracers up the hill. The wind is blowing toward us from the shore and you can smell the smoke of things burning mixed with the acid smell of the powder. It's getting darker now and a small craft is laying a smoke screen between us and the shore. Someone called to send down the bow anchor, and we swing with the wind and watch the shore.

Tokyo Rose just announced over the radio that over sixty percent of our task force of seven hundred vessels were resting on the bottom, round the shores of Okinawa. So far I've seen two wrecks, one here and one at Nago, and the one at Nago looked more like a Jap than one of ours. She's some gal, this Tokyo Rose. At least they play good records along with her broadcasts.

Diary April 21, IE Shima

We'd been watching the island all morning, and the pounding around the eastern end was terrific. Some heavy artillery outfit on a very small island off our stern was giving it hell and great clouds of smoke would completely obliterate the peak. One could see tracer bullets from the 50s, arching from west to east. It all looked confusing to one not knowing what it was all about.

We all wish we had known that lunch today was our last good meal for some time to come. Shortly after two, about forty of us loaded all our gear on our backs and climbed down over the side into a small boat and headed for shore.

All was hustle and bustle up and down the beach for a half mile on either side. Everything with a shallow bottom was nosed into the sand, and material of all kinds was being swung into trucks and ducks and anything else handy. Bulldozers were running up and down, pulling vehicles mired in the sand. All traffic was headed north up through a makeshift road cut in the bluff. Everywhere you looked you saw antiaircraft dug in, and you had the feeling that everything and everybody was on the alert and geared for action.

Our major soon appeared and gave us directions. We were an advance party to set up a bivouac for the battalion, and we headed up either side of the road. On the bluff we came to what was once small farms. Things were pretty messed up—homes were caved in and everything burnable was charred and crumbled. Huge dumps of GI material were piled helter-skelter round about. There were thousands of drums of gasoline and diesel fuel, acres of rations and vehicles—here's where your war bonds are; here's what's making us win this Goddamned war.

Up the road in a bean field, a marine with some cowboy instinct was trying to catch a loose sorrel horse. Jesus! They were tramping all around. What in hell are those? That's right. Japs. Deader than hell. Thirty or forty sprawled in all directions and stinking to heaven. What a grizzly mess!

I'll never forget that hike up the road. After I'd seen the bloated dead woman, all contorted with her hand clutching toward a very small and mangled child, the rest came easy. Almost everywhere I looked, death and destruction and the waste of battle were evident. Jap soldiers, mostly lying stiffly on their backs with joints pulled taut, were everywhere. Equipment and food and junk and wreckage, and the two little kid goats bleating their hearts out in what was once a farmer's hut. But for the stench of death and the brilliant colors, it was hard to realize I wasn't looking at a huge panorama of a movie. We passed an American tank all upended and still smoking, with two medics fishing around in the rags and mangled maggoty flesh of the crew; the stench here was horrible. I found my stomach was doing strange things, and I hadn't noticed both my arms were asleep and blue from the pack straps cutting. My thoughts were centered around the horribleness of the whole stinking business of the world and why man was so beastly. More people should see this. There would be fewer wars.

*Loads of Jap civilians passed us in American vehicles headed
toward a central camp. They all displayed a white cloth about the
head or on sticks like flags, showing they were noncombatants. They
were a dirty-looking lot, dressed in rags. They looked scared as hell.
I saw two old men bowing to some GIs who were pointing in the
general direction of the moving traffic.*

*Further on, a yellow sign guarded by a Negro M.P. stated sim-
ply, "In this spot on the 18th of April, the 77th lost a buddy—Ernie
Pyle shot by snipers."*

*Next, we came to our own dead—blanket covered, lying in
rows, with piles of combat boots in little bunches. GIs and prisoners
alike were digging frantically, as if to beat the smell which was
already pretty bad.*

*We would hear the popping of guns behind us, and M.P.s
along the road told us to spread out because of sniping within the last hour.*

Later—

*We weren't very hungry because we could smell the dead Jap there in the barrow pit.
Hunt and I had gone to get one last look at him before dark. He was shot to hell and had
no face, only puffy hands that clutched his belly, and the maggots—it was so horrible it was
fascinating.*

*We were standing in a group by our first foxholes, newly dug and very shallow, when it
happened. Zing! A red-hot tracer bullet went right between us. I'll never forget the open
mouths and startled expressions on the fellows' faces. Then another. As one man we leaped for
the nearest hole. I found Tropp in mine, but I stayed there cussing him soundly. I kept thinking
about my overexposed fanny. It became suddenly the most important part of me like a girl with
a new bustle. Trapp kept yelling at me to get the hell off him, but I insisted it was my hole and
I'd stay there till we could make some other arrangement.*

*It was a very long half hour, and things had now been quiet for fifteen minutes or so.
We rearranged ourselves and got out the shovels again and really began to make the deepest
hole possible while keeping one eye over each shoulder and both ears fully cocked. Hunt and
I had decided on a double deep one, and we pulled all our gear in on top of us. Lt. Johnson
passed word down the line for us not to get out of our hole, not even to . . . Zing! And it
started again.*

I still don't know how we passed the night. Both Hunt and I shook loose at the joints and our steel helmets banged together constantly. Our friend in the barrow pit was really stinking 'cause the wind changed, or he was getting deader or something. I wondered whether maggots worked at night.

We expected anything, but nothing happened except more bullets. I could feel people prowling and my carbine was ready for come what may. Later, we found out that an eight-man Jap patrol, armed to the teeth, had passed nearby, and the M.P.s down at the civilian camp had killed them all.

EJ BIRD

After all the dead I'd seen, lying scattered like roadkill, bloating, stinking, and covered with flies, it occurred to me that these people were really dead and that it could happen to me at any time. I was kind of skittish the first few weeks from being shot at a couple of times by snipers and having had bombs and heavy shrapnel fall close by. Then it occurred to me that I couldn't do much about it but be careful. If a bullet had my name on it, so be it. I hoped it would be quick. The few Jap soldiers our infantry and marines had missed were holed up in caves, and when they decided to take a shot at me, it became a personal thing. That guy had his sights set on ME, and how close he was and how true his aim determined the outcome. It was much more personal than the bombs and falling shrapnel.

Our battalion was settled midway on the south side of the island, C Company between the main perimeter road and the beach. To the north of us and scattered up the hill were A, B, and Headquarters Companies. Just off the road were our orderly tent, or office, the dayroom, mess hall, laundry, showers, and refrigeration unit. We had two officers' tents and one for me and my clerk. Two-man tents housed the men and were scattered through the rest of our area. In the middle of all this, we had our latrine. None of the above had a wooden floor except the mess hall, which had plank flooring and plywood four feet up on the front, back, and sides. Our electricity was supplied by a small gasoline generator, and the army delivered two hundred and fifty gallons of water each day from a spring below high tide on the north side of the island. We dug a well and pumped filtered seawater for our laundry and showers, using salt-water soap to keep clean. Private John H., our butter, had his own tent. He wasn't about to bathe, even then.

Each man was responsible for his own safety from air raids, shrapnel, and sniper bullets, so just to the side of our tent my clerk and I dug a very special foxhole. I called it my Mormon fruit cellar. It was a hole in the earth nine feet long, seven feet wide, and six feet deep. We left an earth seat along each side. Lengthwise over the hole, we placed a log propped up a foot or so above the center line, then placed pieces of wood braced against our ridgepole. Over this were scraps of metal, then all the earth dug from the hole over the whole thing. We left a small access near the front with a wooden cover to keep out the rain. In a pinch this would hold ten guys, and it was mostly full when the alarm sounded.

Down the road half a mile to the west, Island Headquarters had set up a small tent city to house the displaced civilians. Many of them had been killed or hurt with our initial shelling of the island. These few were the only

"Okinawa – From the Fields"

E J BIRD

"Okinawan Homeless"

ones left, and they were a sorry lot indeed. Our guys called them "gooks." I could not bring myself to look down on them. My feelings were of deep sorrow. These poor people were caught up in a war in which they played no part. They had lost their homes and loved ones, and had dim futures. At the camp they were fed well, deloused, and, as space became available, shipped to the main island of Okinawa where they were setting up a permanent place for them.

I hoped that some of the black-and-white sketches I made would capture some of the misery I saw as they passed our area on the way to the boats. They were carrying the only things they had saved from their homes during the shelling, which was not very much.

Our battalion was there to build and maintain an airfield. When we first came, we found a small landing strip running north and south near the center of our island. This, during the course of our coming, had been bombed and torn up by our shelling, then it had been heavily mined by the enemy. So we cleared all of this, opened a coral pit, hauled coral, leveled and compacted it, then smoothed it into an extended runway. Coral from our pit looked like a coarse white gravel. After hauling over a million cubic yards of it, our bulldozers, rollers, and graders worked it over, and after a few rains came to wet it down, we had a surface that would take the landing impact of our largest bombers. After twenty-seven days we had squadrons of our fighter and small bomber planes moving in, and this was important because it meant we could forestall most of the enemy bombers from blasting our island before they could get to us.

Now that we were settled, I had Nan send me some watercolor paints, small blocks of paper, and a couple of brushes. Art supplies at home were hard to come by, and all she could get was a small school-type set, containing six buttons—the primary colors, black, white, and sepia. That's why, after fifty-five years of hanging on my wall, those I'd framed had lost all the blue. The light had caused it to disappear.

Late spring and summer of 1945 on IE Shima was a wild time for me, and I wasn't too finicky about keeping up my diary, so I'll fill in with some memories.

During our first week while setting up our camp, one of those amphibian rigs came roaring into the area, driven by an African American guy and loaded with lumber, most of it sheets of three-quarter-inch plywood and two-by-four studs. "Where can I find the Engineer Dump?" asked the kid.

"You've found it," I told him. "Unload it over there."

This gave us a good start in building up our camp.

During this time, things were in a very disorganized state on our island. Hunt and I were in the supply tent where I was helping him arrange some of his supplies. Big Money, who was on guard duty patrolling the street fronting our camp, yelled, "Get them gooks! I seen 'em duck into the supply tent." Every rifle in our area began banging away at the tent. Hunt and I both hit the ground, huddling behind some wooden boxes. And the bullets came whizzing over us or smashing into the boxes. We were scared. Hunt started hollering, "We ain't gooks. We're white people! Stop the Goddamn shooting!" It took twenty long minutes to clear things up.

A week or so after we set up our camp, the island was declared "secure." Most of the Jap soldiers had been cleared out, though there were still a few pockets of resistance and stray snipers holed up in caves. I talked to some of our infantry, and they told me there had been nine thousand of the enemy on the four-by-seven-mile island at the start. They had only taken twenty-nine live prisoners—the rest were supposed to have been killed.

Each unit was responsible for burying the dead, both enemy and civilian, in the boundaries of its area. Months later, up by our coral pit, one of our boys stepped back onto a shallow burial site and went up to his knee through a corpse.

After our airfield was operable and we had a night fighter group installed, very few bombers ever made it through to attack us, but they came almost every night at first. They would drop a bomb or two, then go over the main island. If they had anything left on their way back, they'd drop it on us. We were spread pretty thick on our island, so they were bound to hit someone almost every time.

"Okinawa -
Some Lived Like This"

From our area close to the beach, we could see our little harbor clearly. It was maybe a half-mile away to our east and south. We were in full view of some of the action of the kamikaze planes coming down from Japan. I saw several hit our ships. In one instance, I watched two planes flying over our camp very low, so low I could see the pilots clearly. One of our men, a kid from Wyoming, jumped on the half-track positioned near our latrine. He swung the fifty-caliber machine gun and fired a string of bullets. Some actually hit one of the planes and brought it down. I saw it fall into the ocean some five hundred yards out. The other plane kept going, headed for the harbor and the ships. He climbed to maybe a thousand feet. The sky around him was thick with exploding shells, some from shore batteries and some from the ships in the harbor. The plane dove down straight for a cargo ship. At the last minute, he pulled up again and started to climb. A shell caught him squarely, cutting the plane into two pieces, and I watched as the debris fell to the sea. I talked later to some of our navy. The kid in the plane was alive and they pulled him out. He was only fifteen years old.

A couple of days later, another plane got through. This one dived into one of our LSTs in the harbor, cutting the ship almost in two. It was hauled out of the main flow of traffic and beached. I took the captain's jeep and a helper next day to salvage some showerheads and saw the results. We could see the mashed-up plane and the severe damage to the ship. Within a week, there came another kamikaze plane. He circled the harbor and dove into this very same LST.

The food we were given left much to be desired. The first month or so it was K rations. They were awful and came in cardboard packets about the size of a flat pound of margarine. Brown-colored, they were covered with wax for waterproofing and labeled "breakfast" or "dinner" or "supper." Here's what was in "breakfast": on top a three-pack of cigarettes, then three sheets of brown toilet paper, a fruit bar, a small can of scrambled eggs or a container of jam, two or three inedible hardtack biscuits, a pack of instant coffee, and a pack of sugar. For "dinner" they substituted a powdered lemonade or grape drink for the coffee.

This went on way too long until finally we were issued C rations, which were mostly canned things like Spam and Vienna sausages along with dried or powdered eggs and vegetables. C rations were delivered to our mess hall and prepared by the cooks. Even so, it was not much of a step up in the gourmet department. By midsummer, we were getting fresh bread each day, made by a bakery unit somewhere on the island. I lived on the bread and peanut butter for a long time, convinced that much of the C rations were inedible.

Not much changed about the fellows in Company C when we were sent overseas. Bagley was still using our dayroom for his gambling and sending money home each month. Fargnoli, the tailor, found an old pedal-pusher Singer sewing machine in a wrecked farmhouse and sent home for needles, thread, and what he needed to put this machine in operation. I put him on

"Beach at I E Shima"

permanent nighttime guard duty, and he was in business. First, he started making baseball-style caps from discarded uniforms. He took our sizes with a tape measure and charged a dollar. Pretty soon his hats caught on big. Almost everyone on the island had a Fargnoli cap. There was an African American outfit somewhere to the west of us. Fargnoli figured out a way to make zoot suits out of their uniforms; the whole company turned out for inspection one day in zoot suits. He was sending a bundle home each month.

Early on, someone had found six drums of Japanese alcohol in a cave. Somehow most of it filtered into Company C until almost every tent had its own five-gallon jeep can full of the stuff. They mixed it with the lemonade from the K rations and it was palatable. The drinking men in the outfit were in seventh heaven.

Brinton, the AWOL kid, got very drunk one day and decided to kill the captain. He came staggering into the area carrying his rifle, with bandoleers of ammunition hanging from both shoulders, two hand grenades dangling from button holes in his shirt, and a wicked-looking knife attached to his belt. "Where is that peach-pickin' bastard?" he was hollering. "I'm gonna kill the SOB."

My duties as first sergeant required taking care of things like this. It took me almost a half hour, but I finally talked him out of it, getting him to sleep it off in his tent.

Hunt, the supply sergeant, also had his problems with alcohol, except that his reactions were more passive. One night the air-raid buzzer went off, and I ducked into my foxhole. I counted heads. Hunt was missing. I climbed out, hurried to the supply tent, and found him passed out in his bunk. I tried to get him on his feet but wound up carrying him back to my foxhole. During the raid, sure enough, the supply tent was riddled with shrapnel. Even a year and a half after the war was over, usually at four o'clock in the morning, my phone would ring. A drunken Hunt would be blubbering on the other end. "Sarge, you saved my life that night." He would go on and on, sometimes for half an hour, until I'd get disgusted enough to tell him off.

Diary May 6

Saw a Jap plane shot down this morning, a medium bomber. Heard the ship's guns firing in the bay and rushed out of the tent. Puffs of black smoke appeared from nowhere following the plane, and I wondered how he managed to keep going. He headed west, directly above the ships at anchor, insolently, as if thumbing his nose down through the bursts of ack ack. I thought he was going to get the hell out while he was still in one piece, but he did a quick flip, flashing the red balls of the rising sun on his wing tips, and dove hell bent for leather at the largest transport in the bay. God! Did he come! My heart was pounding against my teeth, and I tried not to think of the guys above deck, trying to stop him. He cleared the mast by inches and stood on his tail. I don't blame him for changing his mind about suicide. By now he must have been frantic, and he was doing some very fancy flying trying to dodge, but right in the middle of a barrel roll there was a sharp flash as he broke in two. What was left dropped straight to the water, leaving a thin column of black smoke.

May 8, 1945

I had driven our company's army-style Dodge pickup truck halfway up the island to another outfit on an errand, and I was talking with their first sergeant. "Last night," he said, "a Jap straggler sneaked into the outfit next to us, slit open a tent, and cut a guy's head off while everyone was sleeping. The bastard got clean away. Hey, by the way, I just heard on the radio half an hour ago that the war in Europe is over."

Our war was still going on.

One night soon after that, a Jap bomber got past our night fighters and dropped a string of bombs very close to us. One hit our stacked up gasoline cans in the storage area near our motor pool. The fifty-five-gallon drums of fuel were like bombs. As they exploded they sailed high in the air—huge fireballs spreading flames and destruction. Thinking he could stop it, a soldier from A Company jumped on a nearby bulldozer and tore at the drums to spread them so they would not contact each other. In the confusion, the bulldozer suddenly was set in reverse, and the driver fell off the seat. He was run over and crushed to death.

Diary Notes on IE Shima

It's a very small island. Even on the largest map it's nothing but a pinpoint. Our detailed map shows an island off a western spur of Okinawa about the shape of Robyn's shoe, toe pointing east, with Igusugu Mountain like a bunion on the ball of the foot. It was formed by coral, and is about eight miles long and four wide. Must have been a very lovely place with open fields and sections of palm and pine forests. Scattered about were farmers' huts, made by placing large, flat slabs of coral upright around a pole framework. The roofs were red tile on a mat of bamboo or thatched with straw. Strange tree hedges and walls of coral marked the fields of beans and peanuts and sweet potatoes. Near the center of the island was the village of IE. The map says population five thousand. It looked more like an assemblage of farmers' huts than a town.

When we arrived, there wasn't a building standing whole on the island. A few natives and what few soldiers were left had taken to IE's honeycomb of caves, but most of the people were surrendering to the internment camp just below our area. The fields were ripped and torn and all was wild confusion. Dead Japanese civilians and soldiers were lying all over the place, and our orders were to bury the ones that were in our boundaries.

Our first few weeks were spent ducking sniper bullets. We were armed wherever we went. A number of our drivers were shot at as they drove through the wilder sections, and one

*of the fellows in the battalion was killed as he
was exploring a cave. At night the Japs would
go skulking through our camps, armed with
grenades and rifles, and our guards were given
orders to fire at anything that moved after dark.
Consequently, there was always a very wild time
just after sunset.*

*We saw prisoners enticed out of hiding
by the civilians and by infantry patrols, and we
saw our own dead on stretchers born down the
road in the mornings. The mines were bad and
numerous. Most of them were two hundred fifty
pound bombs, buried inverted with the detona-
tor just above the ground. We lost several men
and vehicles to them.*

"The Way Is Hard"

Years later in Vietnam, our soldiers would experience the form of terror tactics that became
well known as guerilla warfare, but we were subjected to it daily on IE Shima. They couldn't
attack us openly; there weren't enough of them, but they made us very aware of their presence.
Riding in an open jeep toward the airfield and back to camp was a nightmare battle with my
own nerves. Was there a sniper behind that bush? That hill? Up in that tree? Was it my chest he
was aiming at, or that of the man riding next to me? We knew they were there. They'd pulled a
bulldozer off the field and thrown branches over it, not really camouflaging it well, for they'd
wanted us to find it. They wanted us to know they were there, and the next time it might be
our bodies instead of a bulldozer.

I finally stopped worrying about it. If I was meant to die this way, there was nothing I
could do to prevent it, and I didn't want to let the little bastards win, for win they did when I
opened my mind to their terrorism.

One morning I saw a group of twenty or so prisoners. As they scuffled by, I noticed one
was carrying a suitcase, and two carried a third, badly wounded, on a litter. An MP told us the
next morning that upon examination, the suitcase was filled with hand grenades, so they led
the Jap to one side and shot him. It didn't pay to fool with them because they were so tricky. I
guess no one will ever figure out why they are so bent on race suicide. It must be the workings
of a demented mind that would clutch a hand grenade to a soft belly and pull the pin or dive
headlong with a glorious flaming explosion into a bullet-spitting battleship. I've seen the dead

"Refugees"

on both occasions, with scattered bowels and twisted, mangled limbs. One could hardly think of them as human—more like some animal killed by its own ignorance.

As things will, our island progressed, and with progress came roads and runways and men and more men until the whole place suddenly became civilized. We drove fifty miles an hour on the road where once we walked so laboriously. I'll never forget the picture of the Jap civilians watching the power shovel dip and scoop and fill the trucks. Their heads moved with their eyes, glued to the bucket, and in true GI fashion the operator exhibited his skill by maneu-

"The Blind"

vering it with flapping lower jaw straight for them. Of course, he overplayed his hand and lost a very appreciative audience. They always seemed to marvel at the overwhelming amount and efficiency of our equipment. They looked so surprised and bewildered as they watched it roll and churn and grind their peaceful land into one huge fortification.

As the days went by, our concern swung from the snipers to the planes. I imagine, after all the civilians had been moved to Okinawa, that our Japanese population was less than twenty-five.

For awhile, our days and nights were a mad scramble for foxholes. We weren't nearly so afraid of the bombs as we were of our own flack. Most of the Japs that braved our fire didn't even have gas to get back to home bases, but they raised hell when they did get in. Eventually, we had night fighter patrols, and we get most of our action via the shortwave radio belonging to the ninety millimeter by our latrine. However, when the big guns popped and the bombs fell, I would've stacked our gang up against all comers for ability to hit our foxholes.

Diary May 13

Just finished the airstrip. We stood and cheered as they came in. Each group of four planes buzzed the strip and peeled off one by one. Slowly putting their wheels down, they glided in. Our fighters straight from Saipan. Oh, those beautiful bastards!

Just twenty-seven days from our landing on IE Shima. We felt good all of us because deep down inside of us was the thought that we had been a part of something very big. We were standing on our front line, the closest U.S. troops to the Motherland of the Rising Sun, and banging on her door!

Diary May 20

It is very seldom that one is fortunate enough to see the mass migration of a people. It's as if you had the one and only seat at a great performance of a pageant.

I felt very deeply for them, the people of IE Shima. Their homes were gone, their fields were gone, their beasts and fowls were gone, and a part of their people were gone. Only the women and the children and the very old men survived the coming of the war to their land. Even some of these were missing, for we had found them, or rather what was left of them, broken and shattered in the rubble of their homes.

One experienced with them all the sorrow and the misery of a thousand lifetimes of having worked hard and lost everything. They carried with them all they owned in this world and they tendered each box or package or jug with a possessiveness known only to the very poor. In single file they walked, mostly barefoot, in the muddy road, and they chose each step carefully for fear of falling, burdened as they were.

They passed for what seemed hours, and I stood watching them as they struggled forward, without a backward look, toward a new home and a new life.

Today is Robyn's birthday. She's one year old today. I'm so very glad she's safe in our country with Nan, and not exposed to, or a part of, the horrible things I've seen today.

POST MORTUM:

IN OUR BATTALION — ONE MAN KILLED —
SEVEN WOUNDED. DOWN ON THE OTHER
END OF THE ISLAND AT THE BASE
NAVEL HOSPITAL — FIFTEEN KILLED —
MANY SUFFERING FROM SHOCK AND
CONCUSSION.

INCIDENTAL

I WAS STUCK IN THE CULVERT —
WITH GANGER BEHIND ME AND EIGHT
INCHES OF MUD UNDER ME. I WONDERED
HOW I HAD GOT IN THERE SO FAST
WHEN IT TOOK OVER TEN MINUTES OF
GOOD SOUND CUSSING TO GET ME OUT.

Diary May 23

I'd better mention the business of the burning Japanese plane. I was in bed asleep when suddenly I was fully awake and on my feet. There was a great, sucking, whooshing sound, and my tent lit up almost bright as day. My head was filled with the roar, and I could feel the air sucked up around me as it plowed not ten feet overhead. I found myself outside watching the plane like a screaming, red-tailed comet head for the sea. Then a small explosion came, followed by a slash of water. I learned later that a Jap fighter plane had been shot down, and in falling had just barely missed our area and fallen into the sea. Next day, I walked to the beach. I could see the tail of the plane standing in the water twenty-five yards out, and on the beach I found the pilot's rib cage. I got a shovel and buried it in a three-foot hole I dug in the sand.

Sort of a strange feeling standing there in the moonlight, waiting, low-hanging clouds

"To a New Home"

EJBird

and the smokescreen drifting in from the bay, covering everything in an eerie half-night, half-day look, making each object appear shrouded in white candle light.

In the west, we saw flashes of tracer bullets converging on a point in the sky, and later the sound of the guns reached us. The sky in the east lit up, and a low rumble soon followed. Then everything was quiet.

We heard the thin whine of a plane high above us, deepening into a screaming snarl. Our ears split wide open and the fingers of the concussion seemed to clutch us, dragging blood and guts and thought and feeling into a tight little ball inside our throats. Somehow we were in the mud of the ditch when the bomb hit, making the night a sunset and sending the red-hot smoke of the gasoline billowing high. It's right above us on the hill, and we could hear the shouting of the men in the awful stillness.

Slowly the thought and the feeling and the blood crept back to their rightful place, and our minds began speculating on what was happening. As each drum of high-octane gas exploded, the viciousness repeated itself. It was but minutes later when the grapevine brought us the score, but the light from the flames kept on for hours.

"Some Stop
    to Eat"

Post Mortem:

In our battalion: one man killed, seven wounded. Down on the other end of the island at the base naval hospital: fifteen killed, many suffering from shock and concussion.

Incidental:

I was stuck in the culvert with Gauger behind me and eight inches of mud under me. I wondered how I had gotten in there so fast when it took over ten minutes of good sound cussing to get me out.

C Company had its share of southern boys. Among these southern boys were two guitars and a mandolin. B Company boasted a big bass fiddle. This gang would get together several times a week in the dayroom after supper, and country music would whang and twang for hours. I always wondered whether this was actually music, but it was lively.

A short distance up the road was an outdoor amphitheater where they showed movies twice each week. Several of these units were on the island, and the movies rotated from one to the other. One day, the first sergeant from a Puerto Rican outfit came for a visit. He said some

"The Kids Get Tired" and "The Mud Is Deep," right

IE SHIMA
INTERNMENT
CAMP

"They Made Them Wash with Gasoline"

of the guys in his company had formed a musical group, playing native instruments and singing, and that they'd like to come play for us after the movie the following Tuesday. I was sure my whole gang would like to hear them, so I talked it up. Tuesday came, and after the movie, his little band assembled on the platform. They had a guitar, some fancy drums, rattles, stick instruments they banged together, and lots of enthusiasm. The music was far different from that of my dayroom gang, and I thought it was great. My musicians, though, were truly rednecks. Halfway through the first number, one of them hollered, "Play it like Texas," and the others took it up and hollered so loud it drowned out the Puerto Ricans. So much for the finer things.

Diary June 24

Even now, with all our night fighters and radar, some of the bastards get in. Last night one came over the island high. We didn't hear the alert, but the ninetys woke us up, and we scrambled for our shoes in the dark. It's a hell of a feeling to be asleep one minute and the next be halfway to the foxhole.

We were crouching there in the dark when suddenly the whole sky was flaming red, and we felt the jar as the first bomb hit just above us on the hill. Then in quick succession the whole string came straight for us. One hit just fifty yards away and the next almost went down the barrel of the big ninety beside our mess hall. Then all hell broke loose. The ammunition in the gun emplacement started to explode, and we buried our faces in the soft mud while the shrapnel cut the air above us. Thurman was uttering little sharp cries to himself, and Hunt was trying to vomit. We were all scared, and anyone who says he wasn't, lied to everyone but himself.

No human sound came from the gun emplacement, but the explosions kept up a nerve-racking staccato while we shook in the dugout.

"Size
Eight
and
Twelve"

E J Bird

It's strange how quickly news travels. We came clawing to the surface and we knew what had happened. One of our officers, Captain Kidd, and a barber from A Company were killed instantly by flying shrapnel on the hill. Six officers, including our chaplain, were badly injured as they crouched in a shelter. One guard died later. The boys at the ninety were really messed up, thirteen killed outright. This morning we went over to give them a hand, and the things I saw were too horrible to describe. One good thing, they never knew what hit them.

By now, I've grown a callus on my mind. The things we see make us that way or turn us into sniveling hulks with no peace of mind whatever. I know I'm not a brave man, but thank God I have the facility to forget, thus making the whole thing as simple as turning the pages of Goya's Horrors of War.

The bomber had dropped three five-hundred-pound bombs, targeting Headquarters, then A and B Companies. The fourth bomb was dropped a hundred yards or so to the east of us on an antiaircraft artillery unit. The bomb squarely hit one of our big ninety-millimeter guns housed in a revetment, which was a huge pile of earth bermed up all around to protect it. From my foxhole, we were shaken with the concussion of all four bombs, especially the last one. Shells, which had been stored in the revetment, exploded continually for several hours afterward. Toward morning, I took those who were with me in my foxhole to see if we could be of help in cleaning up the mess.

```
IE Shima "Some Ride,
But Most Carry"
```

It was horrible. There had been thirteen guys attending the big gun in the confines of the revetment when the bomb hit. There really wasn't that much left of them. We got thirteen blankets and laid them on the ground. Then we brought out what was left of those killed. We were able to locate body parts of only eight men. The others were declared "missing in action."

One night, Lieutenant Johnson and I were in the orderly tent doing some paperwork. The big guns, both on the island and in the harbor, started firing.

"They Carry
Heavy Burdens"

E J BIRD

A small chunk of metal came sailing through the tent, and we both quickly ducked beneath the long wooden work counter. Then another chunk, very jagged and big as half a cantaloupe, tore through the canvas and buried itself in the wooden countertop.

Even after our infantry and marines had captured Iwo Jima not too far from us, the Japs, still not fully beaten, were like a wounded snake, still dangerous and very much still fighting. Rumors spread that we were preparing an invasion of the main islands of Japan. Then our big bombs dropped and the war was over!

Diary August 15

The poster simply said, "The Japs Quit." This is the day we've all been waiting for! We've heard rumors now for days, but the official news is just a little more satisfying to the peace of mind.

I looked up from my desk to see a colored boy, about two pick handles wide across the shoulders, with an excited look about him. "Sarge," he said, "kin I get me one of them signs that say the Japs quit? Wants it for my guys. We got no signs and I thought . . ."

"Well," says I, "we've just got the one, but . . ."

"Oh, thas okay. My name's Jackson. Did you ever see me fight at Saipan? No? Well, I be damn. But about the sign . . ."

"Well, we've just got the . . ."

"Sure you ain't never seen me fight? Goddamn, am I happy! Been four years."

"No, but . . ."

"Oh, thas okay, Sarge. My name's Jackson. I'm the champ of the South Pacific." He turned to leave, then spun round again. "Goddamn! Here, shake my hand an' don' forget you shook the hand of the South Pacific Champ, the first shake after the Japs quit!"

I'll not forget, not for two or three days. At least, I can still use my fingers.

That evening of August fifteenth, at least on our Island of IE Shima, turned out to be the wildest celebration I'd ever seen. Everything from handheld rifles to the big guns of our artillery and those of the ships in the harbor were rejoicing, filling the air with smoke and jagged shrapnel. I spent the entire night in my foxhole.

A day or so later our fighters were escorting planes carrying the Japanese dignitaries. The planes were painted white, with a big green cross on either side, and they landed on our little field. They were to be taken to the ship where they would sign a peace agreement presided over by our General MacArthur.

Now came the hard part—the waiting. Everyone wanted to go home, to get the hell out, to be free again.

Fellows were going home under a complicated system of points. Points for how long they'd been in the service, for how many battle stars they had (I had one for the battle of the Ryukyus Islands), and other points for things I don't remember. Thus, it was by attrition I began to receive promotions. Within a month or so I had all six stripes of a first sergeant.

"SOMETIMES IT
TAKES TWO"

Diary September, October

We read of strikes at home. We hear of the blundering in our occupation of Germany and Japan. We wonder if our leaders are competent, and we see and feel an utter bewilderment of things about us with all the confusion and confused. My own opinion is that the end of the war caught us all flat-footed. We live on rumors and hope; that's the word, HOPE. We hope everything will turn out all right.

Diary October 9

Nothing like a good old China-sea typhoon unless it's a bombing to quicken the pulse and make the blood run faster. A bomb only drops in one place, once, but a typhoon goes ripping and ranting around, causing no end of destruction, and while the results in both cases are the same, I'll take the bomb any day, because it's over so quickly.

We had the warning and tied down our tents early. All the boats in the harbor took off to keep from being pounded to pieces on the shore.

"Some Had Carts"

Storms were nothing new for us, so we calmly sat while the wind grew louder and more fierce. I would be thinking to myself that it couldn't possibly rain any harder than it was, and then it would come down just twice as fast. The wind blew in gusts and each gust became more powerful. So strong was the wind that it rocked our flimsy buildings and ripped our tents to ribbons. First the roof on the dayroom went, then the tents down through the area. Next the C.P. Tent was ripped and it flapped from the center pole like a battle flag. So strong was the wind and the driving rain that a man couldn't walk against it.

Some of us had taken refuge in the mess hall. As soon as it hit we lost the top tenting, and since it was impossible to move, we hunkered down against one of the four-foot plywood walls to wait it out. We watched the far wall blow apart, but we were lucky, ours held. Some of the fellows took to the old foxholes on the bluff by the beach, and some to the Japanese caves in the hills. It was three days before I could round them all up again.

The typhoon had interfered with our regular shipping of supplies, and we started to hurt for food. We were told the few things that were getting through were given to the American prisoners Japan had released, who were being housed on Okinawa.

A month or two went by, and I recalled that while walking on the beach one day in July I had come upon a wooden crate labeled "Vienna Sausage." I thought at the time that some sailor had slipped by night into the ship's storeroom, grabbed the crate, and thrown it overboard, hoping it would not find its way into their mess room. Like-minded, I went back to our camp, got a shovel, and buried it on the beach. Now it was different. We were really hungry, so I got the shovel again, dug up the crate, and we were fed.

"To a New Home"
and "Where Are
You Going, Mother,"
opposite

Diary October 29

So we leave IE today.

We were up early and hoped we'd beat the rain. Sitting on board the LCT, we watched our island with its lovely mountain fade in the distance. IE Shima had certainly changed in the six months we'd been there, her face scarred with our coral pits and roads and installations. Somehow I felt no regrets at the parting.

Turning the other way, we could see Okinawa and the small island of Sazuko Shima *coming closer and closer. We beached at a place called Hamisaki; why, I don't know. It may have been a town once, but now it was a scattered pile of coral blocks, tile, and burned-out straw from the roofs. Almost like a reception committee, the small-fry Okinawans came a-begging for cigarettes, gum, and candy. We found the whole bunch was willing to settle for a can of C ration. They seemed almost as happy over the deal as we were. It was the horrible kind, called "Beef Stew" by the Army Quartermaster and "that Goddamn stuff" by the GIs.*

The engineers and the Seabees had made some attempt to improve the road as it wound down the west side of the island. It still was very narrow and our heavily loaded trucks had difficulty passing other vehicles and managing some of the turns.

Along the way, and especially to the north, the natives lined the roads. There was a prevalence of old men and boys, each intent upon his own affairs and unmindful of the heavy traffic on the road. They all carried bundles of something or other, mostly on carrying sticks slung across their shoulders. Occasionally, one would look up at us and hold up his hand in a sign of friendliness. There seemed to be no control on the part of the army in confining them to certain areas; they were everywhere.

It was a dusty ride, and as we passed Nago Wan, I recognized a hill I had sketched from the bay in April while aboard the LST. The town was a shambles, but some of the buildings were being utilized by the army and Seabees for various purposes. One had been turned into an Officer's Club and so stated with a sign, "For Officers Only." The GIs were right back at them with "Oki Hotel for Enlisted Men."

We arrived all dusty at our new camp, which was supposed to be all set up for business, around noon. But what business! Only the army could have things screwed up with their special orders. Among other things we had about eighty-five guys I'd never seen or knew belonged to us. Those before us had abandoned the mess hall, the laundry, and shower. It will take weeks to straighten things out completely.

Some Notes On Okinawa

We first learned that the natives are of Chinese and Japanese ancestry and call themselves Okinawan, although they may stem from any one of the several islands. To a student of such things, it would be an easy matter to pick out the Chinese traits from the Japanese influences. To us, though, they are simply natives, some light and some dark skinned, but typically Oriental. In visiting a country, first impressions usually begin with the land, so here is Okinawa:

Hills and hollows and twisting roads comprise a landscape lush with the vegetation of the semi-tropics. Hillsides are terraced to provide space for crops of peanuts, squash, sugarcane, and yams. Yams grow everywhere. The terraces also provide a manmade obstacle course for the beating summer rains and we think of contour farming as something new! They grow bananas here, and rice in the valleys. The hills are pine-covered and trees are twisted by the wind that beats down off the Pacific and the China Sea.

Homes are built with the hurricane in mind. One seldom sees a house or building by itself, but rather a group of buildings in a patio-like arrangement with a border of thickly planted trees or a high rock wall as protection against the wind. The dwelling itself is usually a substantial affair with tile roof and walls of lumber or blocks of quarried coral. The other buildings, thatched with rice straw, open on the court and house the kitchen, goat pens, and odds and ends of sheds. The patio will usually contain a well and a section devoted to threshing rice and grain. A unit like this is complete within itself, but will often be found, with variations, in groups forming a village.

We found goats and pigs and chickens when we came and a few Mongolian ponies used to draw the high-wheeled carts along the roads. A man was rich who owned a horse, for there was always the problem of food to be considered in a land where every inch of space is needed to provide sustenance for the people.

Although farms and gardens predominate as mediums of occupation, we found boats, used for fishing in the quiet bays and coral reefs that bound the islands, for this is, indeed, a meatless place, and a man must eat. Long and sleek are the boats, with room for a dozen men squeezed in. Everybody paddles, or if you prefer, and the wind is right, you set the light square sail to the mast rigged near the bow. Fish spears and nets seem to be the standard in equipment, or one can dive below the surface and seek out the shell fish on the sharp coral bottom.

Although the land is precious, certain portions of it are set aside and dedicated to the dead. One sees tombs, tombs, and more tombs scattered up and down the hills. Elaborate caverns are what they amount to, built to shed the water. A man is known by the way his remains are cared for, or so it seems. If your relatives are very poor, you can expect to find your bones cached out in a cave. They might even go so far as to write your name and a few choice words on the lid of the crock they'd use, but if you were prosperous and left an estate of any magnitude, that is another matter. Great things are planned for you, and a high domed vault is built. The potter is consulted, and you wind up in just about the fanciest bit of crockery conceived by the human mind. I've mentioned the two extremes, but there are many degrees in between.

Now, about the people . . . outwardly their attitude toward us is very pleasant. They cooperate without complaint, and I know of no instance where it has been otherwise.

Surely they must resent our intrusion, but they show no sign. A full-scale war is hard on a land but much harder on a people. The Okinawans seem to accept the situation and revert to the old adage that time will heal everything, and they dig in the ruins of their homes and patches of garden.

They were confused and bewildered when I first saw them. They were scared and had every right to be, for the air was still thick with the smell of death and gunfire. All civilians were hurrying or being hurried to internment camps. Some were in trucks and some afoot, carrying little white flags or pieces of white cloth denoting their civilian intentions. All were afraid their actions might offend, and they would bow at the slightest pretext.

As time went on, we got to know them better. They lost their fear of us and learned our ways, mostly through the small-fry that hung about our heels and watched us at our work. We instinctively liked the kids and would save the candies and gum from our rations to give them. We taught them words, not the kind I'd teach little Robyn at home, but the good old U.S.A. four-letter kind, and we taught them songs, and we bounced them in our jeeps.

The old folks were amazed at us and liked our cigarettes. I often wondered what these people thought as I passed them on the road.

They're moving back to their homes now, and we see them along the highways with their huge burdens. Old men in kimonos make two bundles and sling a pole across their shoulders to carry them. The women are able to walk off with anything that can be lifted and balanced on their heads. Bundles come in all shapes and sizes and may contain anything from priceless possessions to an old squash picked up in a garden. Why, we wonder, are there so many small boys wandering the maze of roads? Where do they live? Where are they going? They weave in and out of the tangled traffic, seemingly leading a charmed life, and will cross in front of a speeding truck like a western jackrabbit. The kids are fond of collecting and wearing GI clothing. I've often wondered what a quartermaster would say to the combination of sailor hat and GI fatigues or of garrison cap and size-twelve combat boots on a size-eight boy.

They're awfully smart, these kids, catching on quickly to the things we show them. They're very likeable, so we want to be friendly. It's strange when you come to think of it; this may be a key to their whole future—this ability to want to learn our way of doing things. Sometime in the near future some historian will set down in better words than these just how much we have accomplished.

Our camp, north of the main city of Naha, was one given over to us by a departing battalion similar to ours at the Kadina Airfield. We had practically the same set-up as we'd had on IE Shima.

One of my staff sergeants was a wheeler-dealer. He had a tent full of stuff he'd bought or traded, like Japanese flags and swords, and for a price he'd get us anything we wanted. One day he came to me and said he'd bought a light ice-cream-making machine from some departing marines for two hundred dollars. He asked if I'd go along with his plan to get back his money and make a few bucks profit. It sounded like a good idea, so during supper that night he got up on a table and told everyone not to leave; he had a treat for them. He'd prearranged for the cooks to whip up a batch of ice cream from supplies that came with C rations. Everybody had a huge helping. Then he got back up on the table and announced that he'd give the machine to the company if they'd each pay him three dollars. That sounded great. He made money, the cooks let it be known in the outfits nearby that ice cream was available if they'd bring in the C ration powder to us, that we'd take half and prepare the other half for them. Everybody was happy and we were getting ice cream almost every night.

With the war being over, there was not much for me to do except to keep the morning reports current, so when convenient, I borrowed the captain's jeep and set out to see some of Okinawa. On one such trip, I drove several of us down to see what was left of the main city of Naha. We found one or two buildings standing in a great pile of rubble. It was a city that once had housed maybe fifty thousand. Nearby Shuri Castle was also rubble. Someone had opened up the main street running through town with a bulldozer. Lath and plaster, glass, tile, wood, and concrete were piled high on either side. It was almost like a two-lane tunnel. While driving I brought the jeep to a sudden stop. Hanging from the debris on my side of the road was a withered human arm and hand. My God! It occurred to me that there had not been enough survivors left in either Naha or Shuri Castle to dig out their dead and wounded.

Another time, I drove a few of my friends to a place where a whole battalion of Japs had committed suicide by jumping from a high cliff. After these four or five months since it had happened, we could see their bones, their hair, and bits of their uniforms scattered among the rocks. It's a creepy feeling to find a withered leg attached to a foot still in a dried-up shoe. On several of these trips, I found a few places I wanted to go back and sketch when I could be alone and could take my time.

It was during this waiting period that we were issued new uniforms for our return home. My tailor, Fargnoli, came to me. "Sarge, you've been good to me and left me pretty much alone so I could do my sewing. Now I want to do something for you. I want you to bring your new outfit to me, and I'll fix it for you."

Well, I did, and he did. He went completely over me with his cloth tape, took the whole uniform apart at the seams and put it all back together for a perfect fit. When I finally got home, I showed up in style.

Diary December 6

Transferred to 842nd E.A. battalion for processing. This God-forsaken rock will soon be far behind!

Of course it rained; it always rains when we move, and we put up our tents, long rows of them. Nobody cared though, for we're on our first leg home.

After three years in the army almost to the day, there's a break in the clouds of my life. The thoughts of Nan and Robyn and the little white house at the end of the road overshadow any discomforts that may come my way. Come rain, come mud, come hell or high water, it won't be long now!

Diary December 22

Goodby, Okinawa!

I'm on my way! It's raining as we sit in the trucks. The ride to Buckner Bay was wet and silent. Everyone in the convoy is satisfied and happy. We're headed home!

Our ship is the "Chenango," a small aircraft carrier. She's one of the "Magic Carpet" craft. She's fast, she's lovely, she's headed for Seattle!

Ship's Log

The Good Ship "Chenango."

Left Buckner Bay, Okinawa   22 Dec. '45
Docked Seattle, Washington   7 Jan. '46

As we waited to board the ship in Okinawa's Buckner Bay, we lined up in long lines, each carrying all our gear. Everyone had his loaded barrack bag and two or three side pieces; we were loaded. I even saw one guy carrying all this stuff, but in addition he was wrestling a huge bass fiddle. One burly first sergeant directly in front of me was no exception. We came to a Red Cross booth, and a pretty blonde woman approached. I heard her say, "Donut, Sergeant?"

The Captain, Officers, and the Crew

of the

U. S. S. Chenango

extend the Season's Greetings

Christmas Day

CHICKEN SOUP WITH RICE

SODA CRACKERS

RIPE AND GREEN OLIVES   SWEET PICKLES

ROAST CHICKEN

GIBLET GRAVY   MASHED POTATOES

CELERY STALKS   SLICED TOMATOES AND LETTUCE

APPLE PIE AND ICE CREAM

ROLLS   BREAD   BUTTER

COFFEE   TOMATO JUICE

CIGARETTES   CIGARS

and he answered without thinking, "Where the f—k would I put it?" Then I saw him turn red.

The *Chenango* had been remodeled to carry one thousand troops homeward bound. The space used to house aircraft below the flight deck now held about nine hundred canvas bunks, stacked three high with two-foot aisles. There were maybe forty bunks in what was once the parachute room, only two high, full-sized, with mattresses. I got one of these due to my rank. The food was tasty, and we rode a storm all the way to Seattle, but no one was seasick, and it was a happy bunch.

As the big ship wound its way slowly up the strait approaching Seattle, I was standing on the flight deck. It was a clear cold day, so clear that I could see the mountains far toward the east. A young lieutenant walked up to me and said, "Sergeant, do you think you could round up a few men to help the officers carry their gear off the ship when we dock?"

Without hesitation I answered, "No, Sir. As I understand it, each man is on his own, and that includes the officers." I figured my army career was almost over, so what the hell!

January 7, 1946

Fort Lawton in Seattle was very much like we'd left it—a place of organized confusion. Its purpose now was to get all the incoming troops off the ships and on to trains bound for their homes in all parts of the country. Those who couldn't board trains directly off the ship were placed in barracks to wait until train transportation was available. I found myself waiting over a week.

During this time I obtained a pass one afternoon, thinking to look up an old friend, Phil Maylan, a well-known Utah sculptor now living in Seattle. When I called his number on the phone, a young lady said he was out but expected at any minute. Would I like to come out to the house? She gave me instructions on which bus to take, and when I got there, Phil still wasn't there, but, "Would you like to wait in the living room? There are magazines. Make yourself comfortable." While sitting there, I could hear voices from the kitchen, then the young lady came to where I was sitting. "Sergeant, could you lend us a hand?" and I followed her into the kitchen.

A sailor was sitting there. He held a gold ring, an earring. They were trying, without success, to punch a hole in his ear with a huge darning needle. "Maybe you can do it," she said.

"I'll try. Do you have a potato?"

She brought one. I cut it in two pieces, swabbed off his ear and the needle with alcohol, placed the flat end of the potato behind his ear to give me leverage, pushed the needle through (ears are real tough). The sailor looked in the mirror he held in his hand, saw the needle through the ear with a drop or two of blood, and fainted!

It just goes to show that my major back in Springfield was right. I was never meant to be a medic.

January 21, 1946
After a train ride to Salt Lake, I found myself in Fort Douglas where I'd started so long ago. I was discharged the next day. God, it was good to be home again!

"Two More Beers"

This was the year I had a double holiday season. We spent Christmas and New Year's aboard the *Chenango*. We celebrated New Year's Eve with fireworks, flares, and rounds of shells fired by the big ship guns. On January first, we crossed the international date line and had New Year's all over again with more flares and guns booming. My sweet wife had held the Christmas tree, presents, and feasting until my return, so I had a second Christmas, too, with my loving family in our little white house.

Some things will never leave my mind, things I saw and felt that were part of World War II: the dead lying there, old men, women, and children, tangled in the rubble of their homes; one young woman, already bloated and covered with flies, reaching for her dead baby; our dead, not yet buried, placed in rows, covered with army blankets, top of the head and stocking feet showing, piles of boots, helmets, and rifles off to one side; the first day, at a crossroads not far from where Ernie Pyle was killed, a young native girl, sitting beside the road weeping softly to herself.

"What's with her?" I asked the nearby MP.

"She was raped," he said. "I saw nine of our infantry boys rape her."

"My God!" I said. "Didn't you do anything to stop them?"

"Why should I? She's only a gook."

Other unforgettable things include the first time I looked at our beach. There was a good half acre of rotting squid lying there, stinking on the sand. They'd been killed when our bombs and shells dropped into the sea. And there was the truck that passed me on the road. The driver had apparently robbed a native burial crypt, for fastened to the truck's grill was a real skull and crossed bones.

One other thing: a new light bomber group was assigned to our airfield on IE Shima. Each of the planes had its own individual talisman painted on the nose or side, usually the picture of a pretty girl, and the girl's name became the name of the plane, like *St. Louis Looey, The Mississippi Chippy, The Dallas Doll,* and so on. One plane was new and a crewmember was propped up against the nose of the plane painting a reclining nude. He had her all blocked in with black lines, and when I first saw him, he was just starting to fill in with full color. When I passed by, all I could see was two full-blown, pink-nippled breasts. First things first, I thought.

Other sights and sounds and smells stayed with me long after the war was over. For instance, there was the sound of an automobile horn that sounded at the beginning of an air attack. It wasn't a special horn; many civilian cars used the very same horn sound. Even five years after coming home, if I heard this particular horn sound on the street, I'd unconsciously start for my foxhole.

I've had a lot of time to think about the war since my discharge in January of 1946. I'm glad I was part of it, but wouldn't want to be part of another. The thing that has stayed with me is the horrible waste I saw, both in life and property. I still see the ten acres of heavy equipment and vehicles we left, all lined up and rusting in a flat field. And I can see the towns and fields of a beautiful country left in ruins, along with the dead woman, her arms outstretched toward her dead baby.

Overleaf: "Some Lost All"

E.J. BIRD

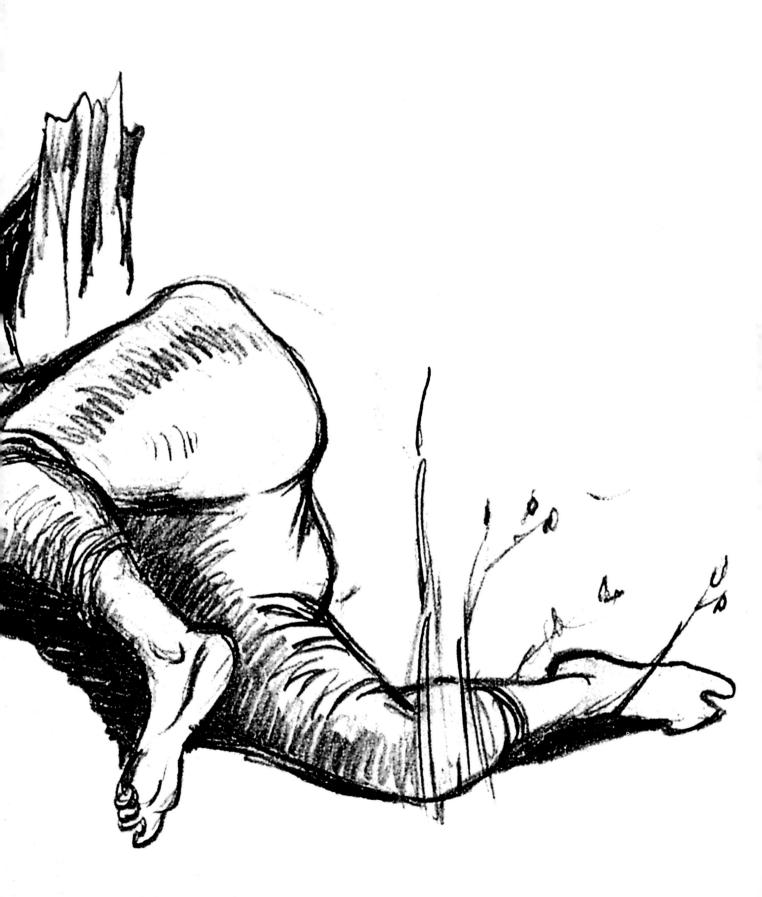

E. J. Bird in
uniform, 1943